English
Olympiad

Class 05

**A must have book for all
Olympiads & Talent Search Exams...**

by
Srishti Agrawal

BLoOM CAP
Bloom Cap Edu Ventures Pvt. Ltd.

Bloom Cap Edu Ventures Pvt. Ltd.

ॐ **Administrative & Production Office**

'Ramchhaya' 4577/15, Agarwal Road, Darya Ganj, New Delhi -110002
Tele: 011- 47630600, 43518550

ॐ **ISBN :** 978-93-25519-24-4

ॐ **PRICE :** ₹100.00

ॐ **PO No :** TXT-XX-XXXXXXX-X-XX

For further information about the books log on to
www.bloomcap.org

Follow us on   

Preface

"Future belongs to those Who prepares for it today"

School Olympiads are National & International level competitions conducted by different Government, Non-Government & Educational Organisations with the purpose of making the children ready to face competitive exams.

The challenging Questions asked in Olympiads motivate them to learn more & more and bring out the best results with improved academic performance. The Awards & Scholarship offered by Olympiads motivate children to aspire & strive for doing better and emerge out to be the best.

English Olympiads

English is one of the most widely spoken languages across the world. In today's era, good command over English is considered as a must have skill. The greatest advantage of studying English is improvement in communication skills along with the growth of personality.

English Olympiads are meant to strengthen students' command over this universal language by improving spellings, grammar, sentence structure and to master student's language skills.

'Bloom English Olympiad Study Book Class 5' is a perfect resource to Study & Practice for Olympiad Exams and other National & State Level Talent Search Exams & Other Competitions.

Some Special Features of Bloom English Olympiad Study Books are;

- Complete coverage of all the aspects of English; Grammar, Reading Comprehension, Writing Skills, Spellings, Vocabulary & Communication Skills.
- Chapterwise Exercises having different types of Objective Questions at par with the Olympiad Level.
- Olympiad Pattern Practice Sets at the end.

This book is prepared by Expert Panel with the utmost care, still if you have any suggestions regarding its improvement then feel free to contact us at olympiads@bloomcap.org. We will try to inculcate your suggestions in the further editions.

Contents

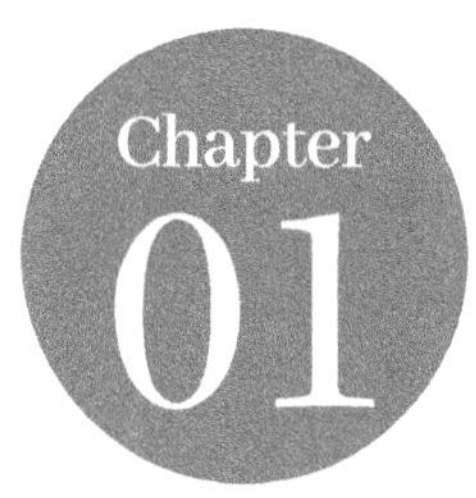

Nouns

1 Mark Questions

Directions (Q. Nos. 1-5) Choose the appropriate noun to complete the sentences.

1. The .... still has not taken our order.
   (a) porter   (b) manager
   (c) waiter   (d) shopkeeper

2. The Nile is the longest of all the ....
   (a) lakes   (b) oceans
   (c) seas   (d) rivers

3. Please remember that ...... time is at 12 noon.
   (a) outlook   (b) lookout
   (c) host   (d) checkout

4. Our players showed great .... in the Test series against Australia.
   (a) reluctance   (b) courage
   (c) bravery   (d) meekness

5. We give a voluntary .... to a campaign of planting trees in every locality.
   (a) justice   (b) social
   (c) patriot   (d) service

Directions (Q. Nos. 6-8) Replace the underlined word with an appropriate noun from the options given below.

6. A <u>herd</u> of birds in flying in the sky.
   (a) Band   (b) Flock
   (c) Swarm   (d) Gang

7. Don't underestimate your own <u>strong</u>.
   (a) Power   (b) Strength
   (c) Force   (d) Energy

8. We waited anxiously for the <u>group</u> to give the verdict.
   (a) Council   (b) Parliament
   (c) Jury   (d) Army

Directions (Q. Nos. 9 and 10) Choose the correct abstract noun of the given words.

9. Succeed
   (a) Succeeded   (b) Success
   (c) Successfully (d) Succeeding

10. Brother
    (a) Brotherly   (b) Brotherhood
    (c) Unity   (d) Society

Directions (Q. Nos. 11-13) Choose the correct option to make a compound noun with the given words.

11. Dining
    (a) Chair   (b) Seat
    (c) Table   (d) Kettle

12. Washing
    (a) Spinner   (b) Table
    (c) Machine   (d) Jar

13. Dry
    (a) Clothes   (b) Hair
    (c) Cleaning   (d) Wash

02

2 Marks Questions

Directions (Q. Nos. 14 and 15) Read the following sentences and choose the correct option on the basis of T (True) ro F (False).

14. A. Beauty is a noun.

B. Beautiful is a noun.

(a) F, F   (b) T, F
(c) F, T   (d) T, T

15. A. Proper nouns start with small letters.

B. Sugar is an uncountable noun.

(a) F, T   (b) T, T
(c) F, F   (d) T, F

16. Which of the following statement(s) is/are correct?

A. 'Junk' is a noun.

B. 'Fiance' is a feminine noun.

C. 'Prudential' is a common noun.

D. 'Jargon' is a countable noun.

Codes

(a) Only A   (b) B and C
(c) A, B and C   (d) None of these

17. Which of the following sentences have the correct usage of nouns.

A. Nutan gave me some advice on how to reduce stress.

B. How much luggages have you got?

C. That's a useful information.

D. The police are offering a ₹1 lakh reward for giving information about the terrorist.

Codes

(a) A and B   (b) B and C
(c) B, C and D   (d) C and D

18. The box has a few nouns listed in it. Select the uncountable nouns from it and choose the option that correctly lists them.

| Cheese | Coffee | Advisor | Envelope |
| Sleep | Crop | Traffic | Plan |

(a) Cheese, Coffee, Advisor and Traffic
(b) Cheese, Coffee and Traffic
(c) Cheese and Coffee
(d) Cheese, Coffee, Advisor, Crop and Traffic

19. Choose the abstract nouns from the given box.

| Charity enthusiasm curious stupidity |
| Honored intelligent humility loyal |

(a) Charity, enthusiasm, stupidity, humility
(b) Curious, enthusiasm, stupidity, loyal
(c) Intelligent, honored, charity, enthusiasm
(d) Loyal, stupidity, intelligent, humility

20. Match the following.

List-I (Masculine)	List- II (Common)
A. Chairman	1. Server
B. Waiter	2. Sibling
C. Host	3. Chairperson
D. Brother	4. Host

Codes

	A	B	C	D		A	B	C	D
(a)	3	2	1	4	(b)	4	1	3	2
(c)	3	1	4	2	(d)	1	2	3	4

21. Which of the following statement(s) is/are correct?

A. 'Junk, Information, water' are uncountable nouns.

B. 'Fiance, person and officer' are feminine nouns.

C. 'Raghav, St. Patrick and Easter' are common nouns.

D. 'Milk, Care and Knowledge' are countable nouns

Codes

(a) Only A   (b) B and C
(c) A, B and C   (d) None of these

22. Match the following.

List- I (Kinds of Nouns)		List-II (Examples)
A. Abstract Noun	1.	Michael Clarke is his mentor.
B. Collective Noun	2.	The bricks are loose on this wall.
C. Material Noun	3.	There is always an incredible crowd that follows me.
D. Common Noun	4.	He was willing to sacrifice his job in order to move to Hawaii.

Codes

	A	B	C	D			A	B	C	D
(a)	3	2	1	4		(b)	4	3	1	2
(c)	3	1	4	2		(d)	1	2	3	4

23. Match the following.

List- I (Types of Gender)	List-II (Example)
A. Masculine	1. City
B. Feminine	2. Cousin
C. Neuter	3. Cow
D. Common	4. Count

Codes

	A	B	C	D			A	B	C	D
(a)	3	2	1	4		(b)	4	3	2	1
(c)	3	1	4	2		(d)	1	2	3	4

24. Which of the following statement(s) is/are correct?

A. 'Common sense' is a noun.

B. 'Thanksgiving' is a proper noun.

C. 'Power' does not have any plural form.

D. 'Actor' is also a neuter gendered noun.

Codes

(a) A and C	(b) B and D
(c) A and B	(d) B and C

25. Which of the following statement(s) is/are correct?

A. Cattle is always a plural noun.

B. Traffic is always a singular noun.

C. Passers-by is the correct plural form of passer-by.

D. Elf is the correct singular form of elves.

Codes

(a) A and B

(b) B and C

(c) C and D

(d) All of the above

Chapter 02

Pronouns

1 Mark Questions

Directions (Q. Nos. 1-10) Fill in the blanks by choosing the correct pronoun.

1. Leena and Payal are very excited because .... are going to Disneyland.
   (a) that (b) those
   (c) there (d) they

2. Mahima and Kajal are doctors and .... profession is very noble.
   (a) her (b) hers
   (c) them (d) their

3. .... wants to go to a hill station for summer vacations.
   (a) Everyone (b) Someone
   (c) Anyone (d) No one

4. One should always keep .... word.
   (a) his (b) her
   (c) their (d) one's

5. .... had been ex-monitors of my class.
   (a) Their (b) Them
   (c) They (d) Those

6. After the accident, Sanjeev is unable to move .... legs.
   (a) those
   (b) his
   (c) its
   (d) himself

7. My sister and .... went to watch a movie yesterday.
   (a) me (b) my
   (c) I (d) her

8. Would you please call ....?
   (a) herself
   (b) hers
   (c) Both (a) and (b)
   (d) None of the above

9. "The children ....work is neat and finished in time will get two marks extra," said the teacher.
   (a) which (b) whose
   (c) that (d) where

10. Did you draw this picture............?
    (a) myself
    (b) itself
    (c) yourself
    (d) himself

Directions (Q. Nos. 11-14) Identify the kind of pronoun underlined in the given sentence.

11. He wants to start his own business.
    (a) Possessive pronoun
    (b) Personal pronoun
    (c) Reflexive pronoun
    (d) Indefinite pronoun

12. <u>Why</u> are you shouting at the servants?
(a) Personal pronoun
(b) Relative pronoun
(c) Demonstrative pronoun
(d) Interrogative pronoun

13. I can't believe it's finally <u>ours</u>.
(a) Reflexive pronoun
(b) Possessive pronoun
(c) Indefinite pronoun
(d) Interrogative pronoun

14. She wants to do everything <u>herself</u>.
(a) Possessive pronoun
(b) Reflexive pronoun
(c) Personal pronoun
(d) Demonstrative pronoun

Directions (Q. Nos. 15-18) Replace the underlined words with the suitable pronoun from the options given below.

15. <u>Rohan</u> did not understand a word of what I said.
(a) Him
(b) His
(c) She
(d) He

16. <u>Baldeagle</u> is an endangered species now.
(a) It
(b) Her
(c) Him
(d) She

17. Probably the captain doesn't expect <u>John and Parikh</u> to finish the work in time.
(a) We
(b) Us
(c) Them
(d) They

18. <u>My family and I</u> are going on a vacation to Singapore.
(a) We
(b) Us
(c) Our
(d) Ourselves

19. Which of the following options contain personal pronouns?
(a) This, that, those, these
(b) What, why, where, how
(c) I, he, she, you, we
(d) Everybody, nobody, somebody, none

20. Which of the following options contain possessive pronouns?
(a) Myself, herself, himself, themselves
(b) Mine, hers, yours, ours
(c) It, he, she, they
(d) Where, why, how

Directions (Q. Nos. 21-24) Complete the passage using pronouns.

One fine morning a gentleman knocked at the door of the home for the aged run by nuns. .....**(21)** ..... told the nun in charge that as he was transferred to Delhi, he wanted to leave .....**(22)** ..... servant-maid to the custody of the nuns. He assured the nun of sending some money every month because .....**(23)**..... was an orphan. The nun consoled .....**(24)**...... saying that she had got an excellent master.

21. (a) She
(b) He
(c) They
(d) You

22. (a) his
(b) her
(c) them
(d) our

23. (a) them
(b) she
(c) they
(d) you

24. (a) her
(b) him
(c) their
(d) his

2 Marks Questions

25. Match the following.

	List I (Nouns)		List II (Pronouns)
A.	Tom and I	1.	It
B.	Heena and Kishan	2.	I
C.	Rohan	3.	We
D.	Table	4.	Them

Codes

	A	B	C	D		A	B	C	D
(a)	1	4	3	2	(b)	3	4	2	1
(c)	4	1	2	3	(d)	2	3	1	4

Directions (Q. Nos. 26-30) Choose the sentences with the correct usage of pronouns in them.

26. A. These gifts are for you and myself.

B. Which is your name?

C. This jacket is not mine.

D. Could you please give me your smart phone?

Codes

(a) A and B   (b) Only B

(c) A and D   (d) Only D

27. A. Sonam and me went to see the Army Day parade.

B. She herself cleaned the dishes.

C. Every of the girls was given a present.

D. I have got any eggs.

Codes

(a) B and C   (b) Only B

(c) C and D   (d) A and B

28. A. He and you should come in the morning.

B. Theirs car is parked in front of her house.

C. I took a leave on Wednesday as my son was unwell.

D. Me and my children went to the park yesterday.

Codes

(a) Only C

(b) A, B and C

(c) C and D

(d) Only D

29. A. They are good at playing basketball.

B. You are the only one which can solve this puzzle.

C. Only those students are eligible to join the contest.

D. Everyone wants to improve themself.

Codes

(a) A and B   (b) B and C

(c) A and C   (d) C and D

30. A. The person sitting by your side is my uncle.

B. The bride started staring at herself in the mirror.

C. She has many chocolates in her pocket.

D. She asked me to complete the project by evening.

Codes

(a) A and B

(b) A and C

(c) Only D

(d) All of the above

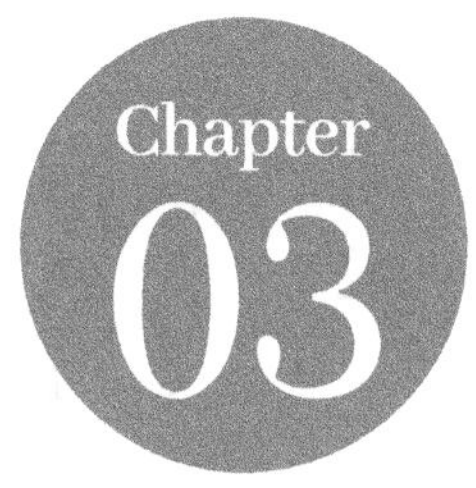

Verbs

1 Mark Questions

Directions (Q. Nos. 1-4) Fill in the blanks with the most suitable option.

1. The girl in the white dress .... my sister.
(a) am
(b) is
(c) are
(d) were

2. They regularly .... cricket in the evening, don't they?
(a) will play
(b) play
(c) plays
(d) played

3. The musicians .... brilliant in their performance.
(a) was
(b) is
(c) were
(d) does

4. She .... the seminar tomorrow.
(a) was attending
(b) attended
(c) will attend
(d) attends

Directions (Q. Nos. 5-10) Choose the correct verb form to replace the underlined word.

5. Disha <u>choose</u> a black dress for herself.
(a) chose
(b) choosed
(c) chosen
(d) choosing

6. Our teacher was <u>hitted</u> by a car yesterday.
(a) hit
(b) hitting
(c) hitten
(d) None of these

7. Roshni <u>builded</u> a new house for her doll.
(a) build
(b) has build
(c) building
(d) built

8. The rally was <u>lead</u> by a senior politician.
(a) led
(b) leaded
(c) leading
(d) None of the above

9. My sister <u>laugh</u> when I told her something funny.
(a) laughing
(b) laughed
(c) laughs
(d) has laugh

10. We <u>go</u> to Darjeeling for a picnic last summer.
(a) gone
(b) went
(c) are going
(d) will go

Directions (Q. Nos. 11-13) The following sentences are divided into four underlined parts marked (a), (b), (c) and (d). Choose the part which contains the verb.

11. <u>I</u> <u>am</u> <u>twenty five</u> <u>years old</u> .
(a) (b)   (c)   (d)

12. <u>Her brother's</u> <u>name</u> <u>is</u> <u>Paul</u>.
(a)   (b) (c) (d)

13. <u>There</u> <u>are</u> <u>twelve students</u> <u>in my class</u>.
(a)   (b)   (c)   (d)

2 Marks Questions

Directions (Q. Nos. 14 and 15) Replace the expression underlined in each sentence by choosing the correct phrasal verb.

14. The gang of robbers <u>escaped</u> taking 5 million pounds.

The gang .... with 5 million pounds.

  (a) get away   (b) sorted out

  (c) got away   (d) put up

15. Manjari says she is going <u>to visit us</u> on Thursday.

Manjari says that she is going to ....
on Thursday.

  (a) hang on   (b) get away

  (c) sort out   (d) drop in

Directions (Q. Nos. 16 and 17) Fill in the blanks in the given sentence by choosing appropriate verb from the options given below.

16. Once I had .... the potatoes, I .... them into half using a knife.

  (a) peeled, sliced

  (b) pealed, dried

  (c) pulled, crushed

  (d) peeled, tore

17. She .... a lot of books and .... pride in it. Look! Even now she .... a story book.

  (a) reads, took, was reading

  (b) read, took, is reading

  (c) reads, takes, is reading

  (d) reads, take, was reading

18. Which of the following sentences have the incorrect usage of verbs?

  A. Can you tell me if Sachin Tendulkar lives here?

  B. The aircraft landed safely on the runway of the IGI Airport.

  C. I look tires today. Don't I?

  D. Naina come up with an excellent idea to help the poor.

Codes

  (a) C and D   (b) A, B and C

  (c) A and C   (d) C and D

19. Which of the following options contain only action verbs?

  (a) Make, warm, go, very

  (b) See, loudly, quickly, think

  (c) Make, go, see, think

  (d) Think, go, very, warm, see

20. Which of the following sentences have the correct usage of verbs?

  A. The teacher make the question paper.

  B. The manager gave her the money.

  C. China is the most densely populated country.

  D. One of the passengers were asked for tomato soup.

Codes

  (a) B and C

  (b) A and C

  (c) Only D

  (d) Only B

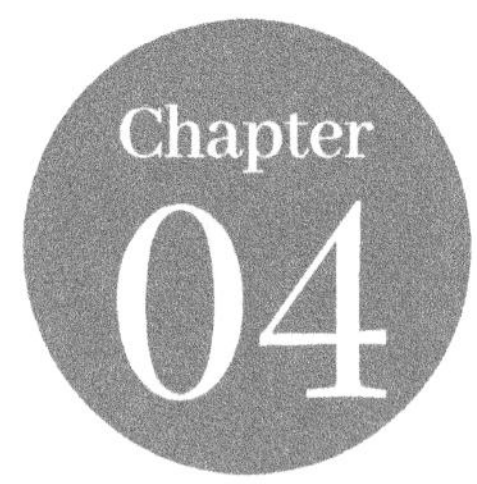

Adverbs

1 Mark Questions

Directions (Q. Nos 1-5) Fill in the blanks by choosing the correct adverb from the given options.

1. It's .... cold today.
   (a) merely (b) real   (c) rarely (d) really

2. The pasta that Mehak cooked was .... delicious.
   (a) completely   (b) quite
   (c) quiet   (d) likely

3. I am sorry. I am .... late.
   (a) very   (b) too
   (c) absolutely   (d) totally

4. E-learning platform have been .... successful in post-covid times.
   (a) largely   (b) hugely
   (c) hardly   (d) severely

5. I reached .... late so I didn't go to the party.
   (a) hugely   (b) very
   (c) many   (d) much

Directions (Q. Nos. 6-10) Replace the word underlined in the following sentences with the appropriate adverb from the options given below.

6. We danced <u>sadly</u> around the school yard.
   (a) Finally   (b) Already
   (c) Merry   (d) Merrily

7. Jyoti has injured her foot so she is walking <u>seriously</u>.
   (a) Clearly   (b) Swiftly
   (c) Slowly   (d) Hardly

8. My friend, Daksha, came to my house <u>tomorrow</u>.
   (a) Afternoon   (b) Friday
   (c) Morning   (d) Yesterday

9. I am <u>highly</u> at home in the mornings.
   (a) Shyly   (b) Ever
   (c) Generally   (d) Fairly

10. The naughty sheep ran <u>bad</u> than its flock.
    (a) Seriously   (b) Little
    (c) Farther   (d) Literally

Directions (Q. Nos. 11-13) Identify the adverbs in the given sentences.

11. She truthfully answered the police officer's questions.
    (a) answered   (b) police
    (c) truthfully   (d) questions

12. The beautifully painted landscape is a wonderful addition to my living room decor.
    (a) painted
    (b) wonderful
    (c) decor
    (d) beautifully

13. The teacher firmly disciplined the students for their misbehaviour.
(a) teacher
(b) disciplined
(c) misbehaviour
(d) firmly

14. Choose the sentence in which adverb has been used correctly.
(a) Namita has been living scarcely.
(b) Namita has been living luxuriously.
(c) Namita has been living last in Delhi.
(d) Namita has been living eagerly

2 Marks Questions

15. Which of the following sentence does NOT use adverbs correctly?
A. They almost forgot about the function.
B. The ship was swifty ruined by the storm.
C. The ship was heavily ruined by the storm.
D. He simply hates sea food.

Codes
(a) Only B
(b) Both A and C
(c) Both B and C
(d) All of these

16. Fill in the blanks in the given passage by choosing the appropriate adverbs from the options.

The night was lit brightly by the moon. I laid .... on my bed. I could see the clouds gliding .... across the sky. There seemed to be peace ....

(a) quietly, smoothly, everywhere
(b) quiet, everywhere, smooth
(c) smoothly, everywhere, quietly
(d) everywhere, smoothly, quiet

17. Match the words given in List I with their adverb forms given in List II.

	List I		List II
A.	Calm	1.	Manfully
B.	Good	2.	Calmly
C.	Man	3.	Temporarily
D.	Temporary	4.	Well

Codes

	A	B	C	D			A	B	C	D
(a)	2	4	3	1		(b)	3	2	1	4
(c)	4	1	3	2		(d)	2	4	1	3

18. Which of the following sentences contain adverbs?
A. I held the handrail tightly with my hand while using the escalator.
B. Is this handwash good enough?
C. Mukta is going abroad permanently.
D. Mintoo didn't take the medicines properly.

Codes
(a) Only D
(b) Only B
(c) A and C
(d) All of these

19. Which of the following sentences have the correct usage of adverbs?
A. Does this train go direct to New Delhi?
B. Apples taste always best when you pick them straight off the tree.
C. Nushrat wrote the address neatly on a piece of paper.
D. As a child Navya was quiet brilliant.

Codes
(a) A and B
(b) B and C
(c) A and C
(d) C and D

20. Which of the following options contain only adverbs?
(a) asleep, upstairs and pushy
(b) upstairs, overseas and commute
(c) nevertheless, upstairs and overseas
(d) nevertheless and upstairs

Adjectives

1 Mark Questions

Directions (Q. Nos. 1-5) Fill in the blanks by choosing the suitable adjective from the options given below.

1. They live in a .... house.
   (a) loveliest   (b) lovelier
   (c) lovely   (d) lovelyful

2. Ramesh is a .... boy.
   (a) modester   (b) modest
   (c) modestest   (d) most modest

3. Bina is an .... baby.
   (a) adored   (b) adore
   (c) adorable   (d) adoring

4. Gold is .... than silver.
   (a) costly   (b) heavy
   (c) costlier   (d) shiny

5. Sally's watch is .... than Mark's.
   (a) expensive   (b) more expensive
   (c) most expensive   (d) None of these

Directions (Q. Nos. 6-10) Replace the words underlined in the sentence with the appropriate adjective from the options given below.

6. Hurricanes have <u>strength</u> winds and sometimes heavy rains.
   (a) Stronger   (b) Strong
   (c) More strong   (d) Most strong

7. <u>This</u> mangoes are ripe, <u>them</u> mangoes are raw.
   (a) These, they   (b) These, those
   (c) That, those   (d) That, they

8. This clown is not as <u>fun</u> as the other one.
   (a) Funnier   (b) Funniest
   (c) Most funnier   (d) Funny

9. The <u>lengthy</u> giraffe is eating green leaves.
   (a) Long   (b) Colourful
   (c) Tall   (d) Green

10. My mother is an <u>beautiful</u> cook.
    (a) Amaze   (b) Excellent
    (c) Useful   (d) Obedient

Directions (Q. Nos. 11 and 12) Fill in the blanks by choosing the correct order of adjectives.

11. What an .... cup and saucer!
    (a) amazing, little, old
    (b) old, little, amazing
    (c) little, amazing, old
    (d) All of the above

12. We took a side of an .... bus.
    (a) Blue, old, Chinese
    (b) Old, blue, Chinese
    (c) Chinese, blue, old
    (d) Chinese, old, blue

Directions (Q. Nos. 13-15) Fill in the blanks by choosing the most appropriate degree of adjective.

13. As we hiked up the hill, our steps got ....
(a) short
(b) shorter
(c) shortest
(d) None of the above

14. My sister wants the music to be .... than it is now.
(a) louder   (b) loud
(c) loudest   (d) None of these

15. There are .... cities in every state and country.
(a) more   (b) much
(c) many   (d) most

2 Marks Questions

Directions (Q. Nos. 16 and 17) Select the statement with the correct use of adjectives.

16. A. He showed much concern for his new teacher.
B. He showed little concern for his new teacher.
C. He showed few concern for his maths teacher.
D. He showed less concern for his maths teacher.

Codes
(a) A and B   (b) Only B
(c) C and D   (d) Only D

17. A. This guy has extraordinary talent.
B. She has made delicious cookies for the party.
C. This door has been closed for a long time.
D. The gorgeous lady is coming towards us.

Codes
(a) Only A   (b) B and C
(c) Only D   (d) All are correct

18. Match the following.

List I (Positive Degree)		List II (Superlative degree)
A.	Big	1. Best
B.	Good	2. Farthest
C.	Beautiful	3. Biggest
D.	Far	4. Most beautiful

Codes

	A	B	C	D		A	B	C	D
(a)	1	3	2	4	(b)	2	4	1	3
(c)	3	1	4	2	(d)	4	2	3	1

19. Identify the adjectives present in the following sentence.

The first half of his debut movie was very interesting.
(a) first and debut
(b) half and debut
(c) first, debut and interesting
(d) debut and interesting

20. Which of the following options contain only adjectives?
(a) Hostile, precautionary, lunar and nuclear
(b) Hostile, precautionary, prolong and nuclear
(c) Precautionary, lunar and nuclear
(d) Lunar, prolong and nuclear

21. Which of the following statements is/are correct?
A. German is not an adjective.
B. 'Suede' is an adjective.
C. 'Abroad' is not an adjective.
D. The superlative form of 'Little' is 'Least'.

Codes
(a) Only A   (b) A and B
(c) C and D   (d) Only D

Directions (Q. Nos. 22-25) Identify the sentences with correct usage of adjectives.

22. A. She wore a beautiful, white wedding dress.
    B. Intelligent people always focus on success.
    C. Give me that big Maths red book.
    D. This week we covered long-term memory in learning psychology.

    Codes
    (a) Only C
    (b) A and B
    (c) A, B and D
    (d) All are correct

23. A. Cristiano Ronaldo is a successful football player.
    B. There are many more beautiful places to see in the world.
    C. The side of the road was full of dried leaves.
    D. Canada is not beautifuller than England.

Codes
(a) A and B
(b) A and C
(c) Only D
(d) B and D

24. A. Have you received the latest news about the match?
    B. There is damp feeling in the air due to heavy rain.
    C. Noki is a muscular woman in this town.
    D. She is wiser than her sister.

    Codes
    (a) B and C
    (b) Only D
    (c) Only A
    (d) All of these

25. A. That house is the oldest in the street.
    B. Buses are cheaper than trains.
    C. No other mountain is as tall as the Mount Everest.

    Codes
    (a) Only A
    (b) Only B
    (c) A and C
    (d) All are correct

Articles

1 Mark Questions

Directions (Q. Nos. 1-11) Fill in the blanks with suitable article from the options given below.

1. .... Tower of London is .... popular tourist place.
   (a) The, a   (b) An, the
   (c) A, an   (d) The, the

2. Where is .... video game I gave you yesterday?
   (a) an   (b) a
   (c) the   (d) No article

3. Binod has .... terrible headache.
   (a) an   (b) a
   (c) the   (d) No article

4. Allahabad is situated on the bank of .... Ganges.
   (a) an   (b) a
   (c) the   (d) No article

5. There is nothing like staying at .... home for relaxation.
   (a) an   (b) a
   (c) the   (d) No article

6. I watched a magic show two days ago which was .... exciting experience.
   (a) the
   (b) a
   (c) an
   (d) No article

7. .... mangoes and .... apples are exported to other countries from India.
   (a) A, the   (b) The, the
   (c) The, a   (d) No articles

8. .... Air India has shown signs of improvement.
   (a) A   (b) An
   (c) The   (d) No article

9. My mother bought .... expensive saree on Mother's Day.
   (a) an   (b) a
   (c) the   (d) No article

10. Look, there is .... little squirrel on this tree!
    (a) an   (b) the
    (c) a   (d) No article

11. I hate .... geography and biology. .... only subject I like is English.
    (a) the/The   (b) No article/The
    c) a/An   (d) the/A

Directions (Q. Nos.12-16) Answer the following questions by filling the blanks with the most appropriate article from the given options.

12. What did you get for your birthday? I got .... lot of good presents.
    (a) a   (b) the
    (c) an   (d) No article

13. Where are you going for your vacations?

I am going to .... hill station in Himachal Pradesh.

(a) an
(b) a
(c) the
(d) No article

14. Do you think your friend is lying?
No, he is the kind of .... guy who never tells lies.

(a) the
(b) an
(c) a
(d) No article

15. How is your grandfather?
He is .... little sick, but it is nothing serious.

(a) an
(b) a
(c) the
(d) No article

16. Where were you last night? I called you so many times.
Oh sorry, ...yesterday I slept early.

(a) the
(b) an
(c) a
(d) No article

17. Which of the following word/phrase uses articles properly?

(a) A Leaning Tower of Pisa

(b) Netherlands

(c) Mile

(d) The Hague

2 Marks Questions

18. Identify the article(s) used in the following sentence.

Every Friday a teacher goes to the prison to teach a maths class.

(a) a, the
(b) the
(c) a, the, the
(d) a, the, a

19. Match List I with List II in order to form meaningful phrases.

	List I		List II
A.	An	1.	most beautiful flower
B.	The	2.	water
C.	A	3.	occasion
D.	No article	4.	frog

Codes

	A	B	C	D		A	B	C	D
(a)	3	2	4	1	(b)	1	2	3	4
(c)	3	1	4	2	(d)	2	3	1	4

Directions (Q. Nos. 20 and 21) Replace the words underlined in the sentence with the appropriate article from the options given below.

20. Right now, <u>an</u> Euro is stronger than <u>a</u> dollar. <u>A</u> rupee is still weak.

(a) A, the, the, a
(b) No articles
(c) An, the, a, the
(d) The, a, the, a

21. Coconuts are <u>the</u> prehistoric plant that scientists believe either came from <u>a</u> South Pacific around New Guinea.
They can be found all over <u>an</u> Pacific, <u>a</u> Indian Ocean regions and Africa.

(a) A, the, a, an
(b) A, the, the, the
(c) The, the, the, an
(d) The, a, a, the

22. Which of the following phrases use articles correctly?

A. A hour

B. The moon

C. An interesting city

D. A Earth

Codes

(a) A and C
(b) B, C and D
(c) B and C
(d) Only A

23. Complete the following passage using articles.

Almost every full moon night, ...(i)... officials in Andaman and Nicobar Islands take part in ...(ii)... cautious ritual. ...(iii)... tribesmen watch from a safe distance as ...**(iv)**... officials approach the island in ...**(v)**... boat carrying gifts for them.

  (i) (a) an   (b) a
      (c) the   (d) No article

 (ii) (a) a   (b) an
      (c) the   (d) No article

(iii) (a) An   (b) The
      (c) A   (d) No article

(iv) (a) the   (b) a
      (c) an   (d) No article

 (v) (a) an   (b) a
      (c) the   (d) No article

Directions (Q. Nos. 24 and 25) Which of the following statement(s) correctly use articles?

24. A. Would you like to come to the home on a Thursday?

B. Yesterday, I bought a blouse and a skirt. The blouse was surprisingly cheap, but the skirt was more expensive.

C. Cats have big eyes that can see in the dark.

D. There has been the previous research on a topic.

Codes
(a) A and B
(b) B and C
(c) C and D
(d) A and C

25. A. After a long day, a cup of tea tastes particularly good.

B. Please give me the hammer and the nail.

C. Eliza will bring a small gift to Sophie's party.

D. Creativity is a valuable quality in children.

Codes
(a) A and C   (b) B and D
(c) Only D   (d) All of these

26. Complete the passage with correct articles.

My mother is ...**(i)**... English teacher. I am ...**(ii)**... student. When I get home from school, I watch ...**(iii)**... programs on TV. That's ...**(iv)**... best part of my day. ...**(v)**... programs I watch are for children. I am ...**(vi)**... child, so I think they are funny.

  (i) (a) A   (b) An
      (c) The   (d) No article

 (ii) (a) A   (b) An
      (c) The   (d) No article

(iii) (a) A   (b) An
      (c) The   (d) No article

(iv) (a) A   (b) An
      (c) The   (d) No article

 (v) (a) A   (b) An
      (c) The   (d) No article

(vi) (a) A   (b) An
      (c) The   (d) No article

Chapter 07

Prepositions

1 Mark Questions

Directions (Q. Nos. 1-9) Fill in the blanks with appropriate preposition to complete the sentences.

1. .... the bungalow, there was an old oak tree where numerous birds had built their nests.
   (a) Under   (b) On
   (c) Inside   (d) Below

2. He was standing on the platform .... the level of the audience.
   (a) under   (b) below
   (c) above   (d) between

3. There was a name plate .... the door of the house bearing the name of the owner.
   (a) at   (b) on
   (c) of   (d) along

4. She had to work hard .... her life.
   (a) through   (b) for
   (c) throughout   (d) across

5. The superfast express arrived at the station .... time.
   (a) at   (b) in
   (c) of   (d) for

6. John was nowhere to be seen .... the time of Christmas.
   (a) from   (b) at
   (c) in   (d) for

7. This restaurant is always in short supply .... food.
   (a) at   (b) of
   (c) off   (d) with

8. I will return home .... four days.
   (a) before   (b) after
   (c) on   (d) around

9. The troops opened the door .... courage.
   (a) for   (b) with   (c) in   (d) over

Directions (Q. Nos. 10-14) Replace the words underlined in the sentences with the appropriate prepositions.

10. We all laughed <u>by</u> the jokes told by Mahi.
    (a) in   (b) with   (c) on   (d) at

11. Rajeev is suffering <u>in</u> malaria for last ten days.
    (a) with   (b) from   (c) by   (d) over

12. Good English cartoons and movies leave a good impression <u>of</u> young children.
    (a) with   (b) upon
    (c) at   (d) after

13. Some people are very keen <u>in</u> working in a team, while others are not.
    (a) on   (b) to
    (c) about   (d) at

14. People who are good <u>with</u> making friends usually work in the field of trade or sales.
    (a) in   (b) to
    (c) at   (d) for

Directions (Q.Nos. 15-20) Identify the prepositions present in the given sentences.

15. Ronny always pays attention to what his teacher is saying.
    (a) to   (b) what
    (c) always   (d) pays

16. Walter is not mean, he is just very careful with money.
    (a) not   (b) very
    (c) with   (d) just

17. Like many other children, my daughter is mad for chocolates.
    (a) other   (b) my
    (c) mad   (d) for

18. I have been waiting for you since seven o'clock.
    (a) been   (b) since
    (c) I   (d) have

19. The artist was insulted by the music director.
    (a) by   (b) the
    (c) is   (d) None of these

20. I felt very sorry for the poor and hungry boy.
    (a) for   (b) and
    (c) very   (d) the

Directions (Q. Nos. 21 and 22) Choose the sentence with the correct usage of prepositions.

21. (a) At least give her credit to trying.
    (b) The club encourages participation at sports activities.
    (c) There has been a lot of resistance about this new law.`
    (d) He felt nothing but hatred for his attacker.

22. (a) There is a real need of discipline in this class.
    (b) I have no desire through discuss the matter further.
    (c) I have a fondness from expensive chocolates.
    (d) His talent behind singing is impressive.

Directions (Q. Nos. 23 and 24) Choose the sentence with the incorrect usage of prepositions.

23. (a) He has the advantage of speaking English fluently.
    (b) I had an argument with the waiter about the bill.
    (c) She has lost her belief in God.
    (d) John left after a quarrel between his wife.

24. (a) A plane is flying above the village.
    (b) We went to see an exhibition of Chinese jewellery.
    (c) The bird flew in the open window.
    (d) He worked throughout the day, and most of the night.

2 Marks Questions

25. Which of the following sentences is/are correct?
    A. At which month does the session begin?
    B. She purchased it from Delhi Haat.
    C. Shoaib got a saree by his sister at some mall.
    D. A gang of wolves started emerging from the west side of the forest.
    Codes
    (a) A and D
    (b) A and C
    (c) B and C
    (d) B and D

26. Match the words in List I with prepositions in List II to make prepositional phrases.

	List I		List II
A.	endowed	1.	from
B.	superior	2.	of
C.	differ	3.	with
D.	boast	4.	to

Codes

	A	B	C	D			A	B	C	D
(a)	3	4	1	2		(b)	4	3	1	2
(c)	2	1	4	3		(d)	1	2	4	3

27. Which of the following options contain only prepositions?

(a) but, or, and, at, yet
(b) across, behind, nevertheless, because
(c) through, more, this, across
(d) under, beside, during, below

Directions (Q. Nos. 28 and 29) Which of the following sentences use prepositions correctly?

28. A. The food is at the table.
B. Where will you be on Independence Day?
C. I have a meeting in Delhi.
D. She was punished for stealing a pen.
Codes
(a) Only A
(b) A and B
(c) B, C and D
(d) All of these

29. A. The napkin is placed beside the plate.
B. Nobody came the party except George and Alex.
C. She came back school a while ago.
D. His bicycle was leaning against the fence.
Codes
(a) A and B
(b) B and C
(c) C and D
(d) All of these

30. Fill in the blanks with correct prepositions.

Mr. Magician is a magician. He performs magic tricks. He is famous .....(i).... his town and he goes to all the children's parties. He performs lots .....(ii)..... magic tricks .....(iii)..... them. He makes all kinds of animals .....(iv)..... balloons. He plays card tricks. His wand flies .....(v)..... our heads.

(i) (a) in   (b) on
    (c) with   (d) from
(ii) (a) on   (b) to
     (c) of   (d) before
(iii) (a) by   (b) from
      (c) under   (d) for
(iv) (a) by   (b) from
     (c) towards   (d) ago
(v) (a) through   (b) among
    (c) over   (d) on

31. Complete the passage with correct preposition.

I sat ...(i).... my bench and put my bag ...(ii).... the table. I opened my book, placed it ...(iii).... of me and waited for my teacher to walk ...(iv).... the class. The teacher came ...(v).... She said, "I saw you all running the garden like wild children.

(i) (a) at   (b) over
    (c) on   (d) in
(ii) (a) in   (b) at
     (c) below   (d) under
(iii) (a) beside   (b) below
      (c) infront   (d) over
(iv) (a) to   (b) into
     (c) for   (d) from
(v) (a) in   (b) into
    (c) of   (d) on

Conjunctions

1 Mark Questions

Directions (Q. Nos. 1-8) Fill in the blanks by choosing the correct conjunctions.

1. .... I shall drive .... I shall take a train.

   (a) Not only ...... but also
   (b) Not ..... but
   (c) Whether ..... or
   (d) Either .... or

2. .... my car .... bike need to be repaired.

   (a) Either .... or   (b) Both .... and
   (c) Not .... but   (d) Whether .... or

3. Come early tomorrow .... we can practise for the annual day.

   (a) and   (b) until
   (c) although   (d) so that

4. We worked continuously .... the teacher asked us to stop.

   (a) unless   (b) although
   (c) until   (d) while

5. He may be talented .... he is very arrogant.

   (a) and
   (b) so that
   (c) yet
   (d) but

6. .... we were very hungry, we did not demand food.

   (a) Until   (b) Yet
   (c) Although   (d) As

7. He did not join us for the movie .... he had already seen it.

   (a) once   (b) though
   (c) although   (d) because

8. Suresh .... his brother is to blame.

   (a) and   (b) if
   (c) or   (d) so

Directions (Q.Nos. 9 and 10) Combine the given sentences with correct conjunctions.

9. Ravish scored good marks. Ravish could not get admission in a good college.

   (a) Ravish scored good marks and he could not get admission in a good college.
   (b) Ravish scored good marks so he could not get admission in a good college.
   (c) Although Ravish scored good marks, he could not get admission in a good college.
   (d) Ravish could not get admission in a good college because he scored good marks.

10. Nutan ate her dinner. Nutan ate her sweet dish.
    - (a) Nutan ate her dinner and Nutan ate her sweet dish.
    - (b) Nutan ate her dinner or She ate her sweet dish.
    - (c) Nutan ate her dinner nor she ate her sweet dish.
    - (d) Nutan ate her sweet dish after she ate her dinner.

Directions (Q. Nos. 11-13) Choose the option which should replace the underlined word to make the sentence correct.

11. They worked hard for the test <u>as though</u> they failed.
    - (a) unless
    - (b) however
    - (c) while
    - (d) yet

12. She goes to the tennis club <u>because</u> she likes to play tennis.
    - (a) though
    - (b) even though
    - (c) although
    - (d) None of these

13. Please look at the map <u>when</u> you'll get lost.
    - (a) if
    - (b) otherwise
    - (c) unless
    - (d) until

Directions (Q. Nos. 14-17) Identify the conjunctions present in the following sentences.

14. We can cook dinner or we can eat just leftovers.
    - (a) we
    - (b) cook
    - (c) or
    - (d) can

15. Jack plays football well yet his favourite sport is cricket.
    - (a) plays
    - (b) cricket
    - (c) well
    - (d) yet

16. We will wait here until the rain stops.
    - (a) until
    - (b) wait
    - (c) will
    - (d) rain

17. Hardly had he reached the stop when the bus started.
    - (a) hardly
    - (b) the
    - (c) when
    - (d) Both (a) and (c)

2 Marks Questions

Directions (Q. Nos. 18-21) Which of the following statement(s) use conjunctions correctly?

18. A. He left the field so of getting hurt.
    B. He left the school because his parents could not pay his fees.
    C. He saved some bread so that he should not go hungry.
    D. She must weep but she will die.
    Codes
    - (a) A and B
    - (b) B and C
    - (c) C and D
    - (d) A and D

19. A. He ran away since he had stolen the money.
    B. Answer the first question before you proceed further.
    C. You will pass unless you work hard.
    D. For you say so I must believe it.
    Codes
    - (a) B and D
    - (b) A and C
    - (c) C and D
    - (d) A and B

20. A. He will not buy a scooter unless you score good marks.
    B. I trust him while he is a trustworthy person.
    C. Maria loves both ice cream for pizza.
    D. She is such a beautiful actress that everyone is her fan.
    Codes
    - (a) A and D
    - (b) A and C
    - (c) B and C
    - (d) B and D

21. A. I started writing while I was eight.

B. They came to talk to me as soon as I entered the classroom.

C. Robin drove the Batmobile where Batman was away.

D. I am allergic to cats, yet I have three of them.

Codes

(a) A and D   (b) B and D
(c) Only B   (d) A and C

22. Match the following to form correlative conjunctions.

List I		List II	
A.	Not only	1.	Nor
B.	Either	2.	Or
C.	Neither	3.	Than
D.	No sooner	4.	But also

Codes

	A	B	C	D		A	B	C	D
(a)	1	3	2	4	(b)	2	4	3	1
(c)	4	2	1	3	(d)	3	1	4	2

Directions (Q. Nos. 23 and 24) Which of the following sentences have incorrect usage of counjunctions.

23. A. Jackson wanted to eat another piece of cake, but he was on a diet.

B. His two favourite sports are football and tennis.

C. Neither the children or the parents attended the function.

D. This car has been in my house once my childhood.

Codes

(a) Only C   (b) A and D
(c) A and B   (d) C and D

24. A. We had no sooner gone to bed than the phone rang.

B. Mary not only but also Gabriel is from Italy.

C. He felt so angry that he threw all the stuff away.

D. She started to learn yoga, whether she wanted to learn how to relax.

Codes

(a) Only C   (b) Only B
(c) B and D   (d) A and C

25. Complete the following passage using suitable conjunctions.

Everyone needs quality sleep every single night, ...(i)..... lifestyle choices and hurdles make sleep disorders more common than good sleep. This poor sleeping pattern has serious affects on our health, ...(ii).... the first thing we notice is unhealthy weight gain ....(iii) ..... weight loss, low concentration, and mood swings. If you have trouble sleeping almost every day and this lack of sleep is affecting your day to-day routine, ...(iv)..... you may be suffering from one of the many (and most common) sleep disorders.

(i) (a) But   (b) And
    (c) Yet   (d) Or

(ii) (a) Or   (b) And
    (c) So   (d) Because

(iii) (a) Than   (b) After
    (c) Before   (d) Or

(iv) (a) Than   (b) Then
    (c) Although   (d) Since

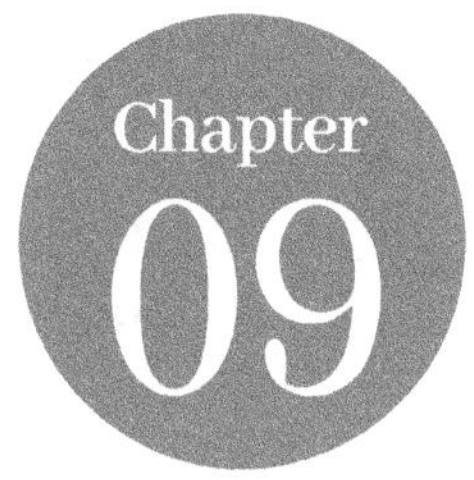

Sentences

1 Mark Questions

Directions (Q. Nos. 1-5) Choose the sentence which is grammatically correct and meaningful.

1. (a) Although she complete her literature review, she still needed to work on her methods section.
   (b) Because he organised his sources by theme, it was easier from his readers to follow.
   (c) They studied APA rules for many hours as they were so interesting.
   (d) I always wanted to become a writer, and she wants to became a doctor.

2. (a) Their plots were failing because of some trusted friends of the king.
   (b) War do not bring anything good to the common people.
   (c) I went to the tea stall for ordered a cup of tea.
   (d) We knows the value of trees but we are falling them unnecessarily.

3. (a) Either Mohan nor his friends have made this mischief.
   (b) As I have fever today, I cannot attend college.
   (c) I know that you always wants to be a writer.
   (d) When you are going to submit your assignment?

4. (a) How disgusting it become when he open his mouth!
   (b) Could you please help me with these bag?
   (c) Don't be excited about everything with reason.
   (d) May you two live long enough to see your grandchildren.

5. (a) Please forgive my meticulousness but you have spelled it wrong.
   (b) Abha feels awkward as someone gives a compliment to her.
   (c) Eventually, they succeeded in his plan of killing the king.
   (d) How on earth did you thinks about me in that way?

Directions (Q. Nos. 6-8) Identify the subject of the following sentences.

6. The cat ran after the mouse.
   (a) The mouse
   (b) ran after
   (c) ran after the mouse
   (d) The cat

7. There were three stray puppies near our house today.
   (a) There were
   (b) near our house today
   (c) three stray puppies
   (d) puppies

8. Shivani fought against all the odds of life and became successful.
(a) Shivani
(b) Fought against
(c) Became successful
(d) Shivani fought against all the odds

Directions (Q. Nos. 9 and 10) Identify the predicates of the following sentences.

9. Suman spoiled the painting by folding it.
(a) Suman
(b) the painting by folding it
(c) Suman spoiled
(d) spoiled the painting by folding it

10. Actors, leaders and businessmen participated in the protest march.
(a) Actors, leaders and farmers
(b) participated in the protest march
(c) businessmen participated in the protest march
(d) and businessmen participated in the protest march

Directions (Q. Nos. 11 and 12) Identify the object in the following sentences.

11. The teacher wrote the summary on the whiteboard.
(a) The teacher
(b) the summary
(c) the whiteboard
(d) 'the summary' and 'the whiteboard'

12. Ustad Bismillah Khan played the shehnai at the concert.
(a) the concert
(b) played
(c) Ustad Bismillah Khan
(d) the shehnai

Directions (Q.Nos. 13 and 14) Fill in the blanks to form complete sentence.

13. His scorecard was not as .... I thought.
(a) worst
(b) good like
(c) worse
(d) bad as

14. The old man lived ...... than 100 years.
(a) for more
(b) for many
(c) for much
(d) for some

2 Marks Questions

15. Match the following to form meaningful sentences.

	List I		List II
A.	Let me know if	1.	planes are landing.
B.	In spite of the fog.	2.	you go to the school.
C.	I hope	3.	out with strangers.
D.	He loves hanging	4.	you can come tomorrow.

Codes

	A	B	C	D		A	B	C	D
(a)	3	1	4	2	(b)	4	2	3	1
(c)	2	1	4	3	(d)	1	4	3	2

Directions (Q. Nos. 16 and 17) Which of the following is/are meaningful sentences?

16. A. His mother raised him to be a gentleman.
B. Sharmila is always humble and patient with her fans.
C. The train leave every morning at 8 o'clock.
D. I have many money at the moment.
Codes
(a) A and B
(b) A and D
(c) C and D
(d) B and C

17. A. Shall we eat our dinner now?

    B. You have to work hard to be the best goalkeeper.

    C. Books can taught us a lot of things.

    D. The fact that my father took the computer away was a sign that he was angry.

Codes

(a) Only D   (b) A and D

(c) Only C   (d) A, B and D

Directions (Q. Nos. 18 and 19) Read the following sentences and choose the sentence with correct marking of subject and predicate.

18. P : Neel (sub)/ has to go to the airport to pick his parents up. (pre)

    Q : My father is (sub)/ sleeping. (pre)

    R : I (sub)/ will not tell you the secret of this magic trick. (pre)

    S : Vani (sub)/ and her mother are going to the market to buy clothes. (pre)

Codes

(a) P and S   (b) Only R

(c) P and R   (d) Only Q

19. P : The Earth completes (sub)/ one revolution around the Sun in 365 days. (pre)

    Q : We had a (sub)/ three-course meal yesterday. (pre)

    R : Jenny and I (sub)/ opened all the gifts. (pre)

    S : Our guests (sub)/ were happy by our hospitality. (pre)

Codes

(a) P and Q   (b) R and S

(c) P and R   (d) Q and S

20. Which of the following is/are NOT meaningful sentences?

    A : The cat is sleeping on the couch.

    B : When he is young, he lose his favourite toy.

    C : He plays the trumpet and she plays the piano.

    D : They can listening to music provided they disturbed nobody.

Codes

(a) B and D

(b) A and C

(c) A and D

(d) B and C

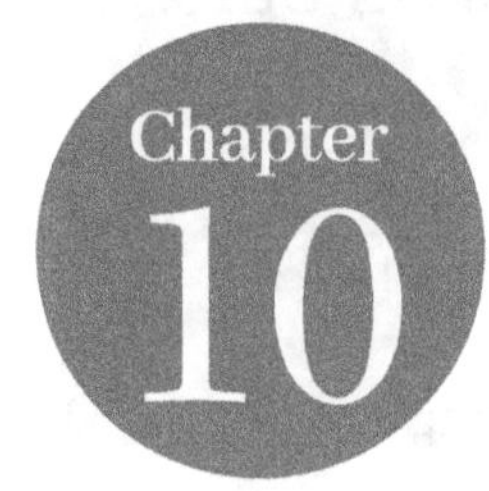

Chapter 10

Tenses

1 Mark Questions

Directions (Q. Nos. 1-5) In the following sentences, fill in the blanks by choosing the correct option.

1. Look! Sara .... to see a movie.
   (a) go   (b) went
   (c) is going   (d) will be going

2. In her right hand, Sara .... her hand bag.
   (a) is carrying   (b) carried
   (c) carries   (d) All of these

3. The handbag .... really beautiful.
   (a) is   (b) was
   (c) Both (a) and (b) (d) None of these

4. Sara usually .... on black shoes but today she .... white trainers.
   (a) put, wears   (b) puts, is wearing
   (c) put, was wearing (d) put, were

5. Look! She is .... an umbrella as it is ....
   (a) takes, raining   (b) taking, raining
   (c) look, raining   (d) None of these

Directions (Q Nos. 6-8) Complete the conversation by choosing the correct verbs to fill in the blanks.

6. Rashu : Why did you go to London?

   Avni : We ...... to London because our friend ...... us.

   (a) go, has
   (b) went, had invited
   (c) going, has been invited
   (d) went, has invited

7. Manager   : How many pages did Jane type?

   Receptionist : Jane .... already typed three pages when her computer ....

   (a) have, crashed   (b) has, crashing
   (c) had, crashed   (d) is, crashing

8. Peehu   : When did you lose your camera?

   Sambhav : I think I lost my camera when I .... down from the taxi.

   (a) got   (b) gotten
   (c) was running   (d) was getting

Directions (Q. Nos. 9 and 10) Replace the underlined word to make a grammatically correct sentence.

9. She finally <u>finish</u> her holiday homework before the school reopened.
   (a) finish   (b) finished
   (c) will finish   (d) finishing

10. My brother <u>work</u> in a Multi-National Company (MNC).
    (a) will working   (b) will worked
    (c) works   (d) has working

11. Change the given sentence into past continuous tense.

I am playing the piano.
(a) I was playing the piano.
(b) I played the piano.
(c) I will be playing the piano.
(d) I have played the piano.

12. Change the given sentence into future perfect tense.

I have studied for three hours.
(a) I will study for three hours.
(b) I will have studied for three hours.
(c) I will be studying for three hours.
(d) I have been studying for three hours.

Directions (Q. Nos. 13 and 14) Identify the tense used in the following sentence.

13. My boss left for London yesterday.
(a) Simple Present tense
(b) Present Continuous tense
(c) Simple Past tense
(d) None of the above

14. Since it had been snowing, many trains were cancelled.
(a) Simple Past tense
(b) Past continuous tense
(c) Past Perfect Continuous tense
(d) Past Perfect tense

Directions (Q. Nos. 15 and 16) In each of the questions, select the option with the correct use of tense.

15. (a) I visit my grandmother every weekend.
(b) I visiting my grandmother every weekend.
(c) I has visited my grandmother every weekend.
(d) I will be visit my grandmother every weekend.

16. (a) He is plant a sapling in the garden.
(b) He planting a sapling in the garden.
(c) He planted a sapling in the garden.
(d) He have planted a sapling in the garden.

2 Marks Questions

17. Consider the following sentences.
1. Samara went office to get her coat and came back after dinner.
2. The boys are learning Spanish right now.
3. She is constantly changing her hair colour.

Which of these statements are in present continuous tense?
(a) 1 and 2   (b) 1 and 3
(c) 2 and 3   (d) All of these

18. Which of these statements is/are examples of future continuous tense?

A. John will have been running a marathon this Monday.
B. What will you be doing when I arrive?
C. It will net rain this time tomorrow.
D. The children will be sleeping till late on Thursday.

Codes
(a) A and C   (b) Only D
(c) B and D   (d) Only A

Directions (Q. Nos. 19 and 20) Match the sentences with their correct forms of tenses.

19.

	List I (Sentence)		List II (Tense)
A.	I need a pair of new boots.	1.	Simple Past
B.	He had repeated the test and got a better score.	2.	Present Continuous

	List I (Sentence)	List II (Tense)
C.	Did your mother work in a restaurant?	3. Simple Present
D.	I am presently enjoying my summer holidays.	4. Past Perfect

Codes

	A	B	C	D
(a)	2	3	1	4
(b)	3	1	2	4
(c)	3	4	1	2
(d)	2	4	1	3

20.

	List I (Sentence)	List II (Tense)
A.	She will join a new company next month.	1. Present Perfect
B.	I will be cooking food for 10 people tomorrow.	2. Present Perfect Continuous
C.	They have not received any payment for the work.	3. Future Continuous
D.	He has not been washing his clothes.	4. Simple Future

Codes

	A	B	C	D		A	B	C	D
(a)	4	3	1	2	(b)	3	2	4	1
(c)	2	1	3	4	(d)	1	3	2	4

21. Read the passage given below and fill in the blanks with verbs in proper tense from the options given below.

The Universe is everything we can touch, feel, sense, measure or detect. It .... living things, planets, stars, galaxies, light and even time. The Universe is huge, but it .... this big. Scientists believe it began in a Big Bang. Which .... place nearly 14 billion years ago. Since then, the Universe has been .... outward at a very high speed.

(a) includes, has not always been, took, expanding

(b) included, had always been, take, expanded

(c) includes, had not always been, taken, expands

(d) included, has always been, takes, expand

Directions (Q. Nos. 22 and 23) Choose the sentence(s) which is/are in future perfect tense.

22. A. The boys have prepared for their exam.

    B. You will have studied the English language by the age of 5.

    C. I will not have received any reply from him.

    D. They had invited their friends to their party.

Codes

(a) Only A   (b) A and B

(c) B and C   (d) Only D

23. A. She will have studied hard during the exam.

    B. He will have lost all the money in three days.

    C. They will have woken early in the morning.

    D. Dad will not have gone to London next week.

Codes

(a) A and B

(b) C and D

(c) A, C and D

(d) All of the above

Directions (Q. Nos. 24 and 25) Choose the sentences which are NOT in past perfect tense.

24. A. The boys had prepared for their exam.
    B. I have told you that you should go there.
    C. The girls had rehearsed well.
    D. She had been cooking food for two years.
    Codes
    (a) A and B
    (b) B and C
    (c) A and C
    (d) B and D

25. A. He will not have been going to the airport before 10 o'clock.
    B. I am going to swimming classes these days.
    C. She had met him before the party.
    D. I had written the email before he apologised.
    Codes
    (a) A and B
    (b) Only C

(c) B, C and D
(d) All of the above are in Past Perfect Tense

Directions (Q. Nos. 26 and 27) Choose the sentence which are in present perfect continuous tense.

26. A. We've been studying since 9 o'clock.
    B. I am helping him to do the task.
    C. I was not sleeping when you got home late last night.
    D. Tara hasn't been feeling well for two weeks.
    Codes
    (a) A and B   (b) B and C
    (c) C and D   (d) A and D

27. A. We hadn't been living there long.
    B. We hadn't been studying very hard.
    C. Are you listening to realistic songs?
    D. I am not quarreling with you.
    Codes
    (a) A and B
    (b) B and C
    (c) C and D
    (d) None of the above

Punctuations

1 Mark Questions

Directions (Q. Nos. 1-9) In the questions given below, select the option which is correctly punctuated.

1. (a) She didnt hear the childrens cries.
   (b) She didnt hear the children's cries.
   (c) She didn't hear the childrens cries.
   (d) She didn't hear the children's cries.

2. (a) The dogs bark was far worse than it's bite.
   (b) The dog's bark was far worse than it's bite.
   (c) The dog's bark was far worse than its bite.
   (d) The dogs bark was far worse than it's bite.

3. (a) Didn't you hear that I am leaving now?
   (b) Didn't you hear that I am leaving now!
   (c) Didn't you hear that I m leaving now.
   (d) Didn't you hear that I am leaving. Now!

4. (a) Butter which is lighter than water, floats on it's surface.
   (b) Butter, which is lighter than water, floats on its surface.
   (c) Butter, which is lighter than water, floats on it's surface.
   (d) Butter which is lighter than water floats on it's surface.

5. (a) Can we leave the room Miss!
   (b) Can we leave the Room. Miss!
   (c) Can we leave the Room, Miss!
   (d) Can we leave the room, Miss?

6. (a) "There are three more cup cakes", the teacher said.
   (b) There are "three more cup cakes" the teacher said.
   (c) There are three more cup cakes, "the teacher" said.
   (d) There are "three" more cup cakes the Teacher said.

7. (a) Steven shouted, "I don't want" to clean my room.
   (b) Steven shouted, "I don't want to clean my room."
   (c) Steven shouted, I don't want to "clean my room."
   (d) Steven shouted, I don't want to clean "my room."

8. (a) I said that she is intelligent not pretty.
   (b) I said that she is, intelligent not pretty.
   (c) I said that, she is intelligent not pretty.
   (d) I said that she is intelligent, not pretty.

9. (a) I have been to France-Germany-China and Spain.
   (b) I have been to France-Germany, China and Spain.
   (c) I have been to France, Germany, China and Spain.
   (d) I have been to France; Germany; China and Spain.

Directions (Q. Nos. 10 and 11) In the following questions, choose the appropriate punctuation mark for the sentence.

10. I think it is going to rain tomorrow
    (a) Full stop (.)
    (b) Exclamation mark (!)
    (c) Question mark (?)
    (d) Comma (,)

11. When are you going to take out the trash
    (a) Exclamation mark (!)
    (b) Question mark (?)
    (c) Full stop (.)
    (d) Capital letter

Directions (Q. Nos. 12 and 13) Choose the correct option to select the word that needs a capital letter in the sentence.

12. disha and neelu are very close friends.
    (a) disha   (b) neelu
    (c) friends   (d) Both (a) and (b)

13. sunil gavaskar's son has also joined the national cricket team.
    (a) son
    (b) sunil gavaskar's
    (c) national
    (d) None of the above

14. Select the option which corrects the mistake in the use of apostrophe in the given sentence.
    Mr. John's daughter is my daughters best friend.
    (a) Johns   (b) friend's
    (c) daughter's   (d) Both (a) and (c)

2 Marks Questions

15. Fill in the blanks with correct punctuation marks to make the sentences meaningful.

    What a pleasant day it was ...**(i)**... Shalini, Ahana ...**(ii)**... Rashi and Garima were playing in the ground.
    (i) (a) Exclamation mark (!)
        (b) Full stop (.)
        (c) Question mark (?)
        (d) None of the above
    (ii) (a) Colon (:)   (b) Semi colon (;)
         (c) Apostrophe (') (d) Comma (,)

16. Which of the following sentence(s) is/are properly punctuated?
    A. She said, "I do not agree with you."
    B. Did you do your homework?
    C. I havent seen you since ages!
    D. How! what a beautiful car it is
    Codes
    (a) Only A   (b) A and B
    (c) A, C and D   (d) None of these

Directions (Q. Nos. 17 and 18) Which of the following sentences are NOT properly punctuated?

17. A. In what way is an ant different from a spider.
    B. Many farmers are protesting at the border against the new farm laws.
    C. The weather is awful today.
    D. Is it necessary to agree to the PM.
    Codes
    (a) A and B   (b) B and C
    (c) C and D   (d) A and D

18. A. Are you ready for the magic.
    B. Joy is a good for nothing fellow.
    C. Ratan Tata is a philanthropist. Isn't he.
    D. What is the difference between a verb and a noun!
    Codes
    (a) A and B
    (b) B and C
    (c) A and D
    (d) A, C and D

19. Choose the correct option after matching the sentences with the appropriate punctuation marks.

	List I (Sentence)		List II (Punctuation mark)
A.	When is your birthday (…)	1.	Full stop
B.	Wow (…) This ice cream is my favourite.	2.	Comma
C.	The cat jumped on the fence (…)	3.	Exclamation mark
D.	I bought a juicy apple (…) a mango and a ripe banana.	4.	Question mark

Codes

	A	B	C	D
(a)	3	1	2	4
(b)	4	3	1	2
(c)	2	3	1	4
(d)	1	3	4	2

20. Consider the following statements.

1. Let's go to the library to study; it's the only place where I can fully concentrate.
2. The butcher told us. We are, "closing at 7 o'clock."
3. Wow! It is really cold outside!

Which of these sentences are correctly punctuated?

(a) 1 and 2   (b) 2 and 3
(c) 1 and 3   (d) All of these

Directions (Q. Nos. 21 and 22) Choose the sentences which are correctly punctuated.

21. A. He always loved sweets, chocolates, biscuits and peppermints.
B. "Clean your feet before you enter" said his sister.
C. They left Bangalore, India on January 18 of that year.
D. I stay in Bangalore Karnataka India.
Codes
(a) A and B   (b) B and C
(c) A and C   (d) B and D

22. A. The minister said, "Elections will be held in MP, Bihar and Odisha."
B. Carlos asked, "Did you get the answer to number six?"
C. The lead prosecutor was prepared, however, for a situation like this.
D. Hari, my brother, is about to reach Mumbai.
Codes
(a) A and C
(b) B and C
(c) C and D
(d) All of the above

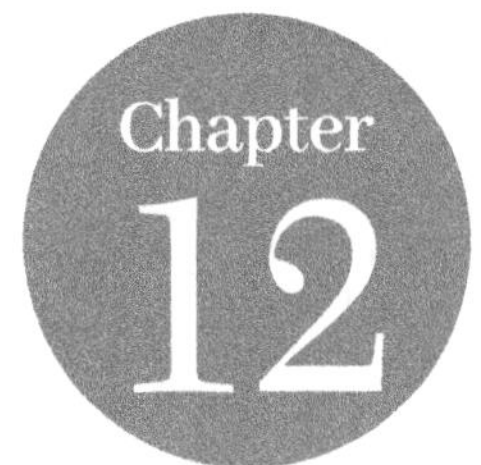

Chapter 12

Active and Passive Voice

Directions (Q. Nos. 1-5) Fill in the blanks to form these sentences in passive voice.

1. English .... all over the world.
   (a) is speak   (b) is spoke
   (c) is spoken   (d) None of these

2. All the school rooms .... by the staff daily.
   (a) is cleaned   (b) are cleaned
   (c) was cleaned   (d) None of these

3. All the files .... neatly .... by my peon.
   (a) is/kept   (b) are/kept
   (c) was/kept   (d) None of these

4. A letter .... by to his aunt by him.
   (a) is being written (b) is wrote
   (c) is writing   (d) are written

5. New cars .... by the thieves.
   (a) is stolen   (b) was stolen
   (c) were stolen   (d) None of these

Directions (Q. Nos. 6-10) Choose the correct option that would replace the underlined verb to rewrite the following sentences in passive forms.

6. Lakhs of people <u>celebrated</u> International Yoga day on 21st June all over the world.

   International Yoga day .... on 21st June by lakhs of people all over the world.
   (a) is celebrated
   (b) is being celebrated
   (c) was celebrated
   (d) celebrated

7. Thieves <u>held</u> the manager of the Claridges Hotel at gunpoint yesterday.

   The manager of the Claridges Hotel .... at gun point by thieves yesterday.
   (a) was held
   (b) were held
   (c) is being held
   (d) is held

8. The thieves <u>took away</u> around 50 lakh rupees from the hotel's safe.

   Around 50 lakh rupees .... by the thieves from the hotel's safe.
   (a) was taken away
   (b) is taken away
   (c) were taken away
   (d) None of the above

9. The Prime Minister <u>refused</u> selfies on Yoga day.

   Selfies on Yoga day .... by the Prime Minister.
   (a) are refused
   (b) was refused
   (c) is refused
   (d) were refused

10. Hundreds of nurses in the UK <u>face</u> deportation.

Deportation .... by hundreds of nurses in the UK.
(a) was faced (b) is faced
(c) were being faced (d) None of these

Directions (Q. Nos. 11-16) Change the voice of the following sentences.

11. My uncle will review the case.
(a) The case is being reviewed by my uncle.
(b) My uncle reviewed the case.
(c) The case will be reviewed by my uncle.
(d) The case has been reviewed by my uncle.

12. Karina squeezed the toothpaste with all her strength.
(a) The toothpaste was squeezed with all her strength by Karina.
(b) The toothpaste has been squeezed with all her strength by Karina.
(c) The toothpaste had been squeezed with all her strength by Karina.
(d) The toothpaste will be squeezed with all her strength by Karina.

13. Who taught you English?
(a) By whom were you taught English?
(b) By whom has you taught English?
(c) By whom have you taught English?
(d) By whom had you taught English?

14. The host received guests in the reception area.
(a) Guests have received by the host in the reception area.
(b) Guests had received by the host in the reception area.
(c) Guests have receive by the host in the reception area.
(d) Guests were received by the host in the reception area.

15. By whom was the job done?
(a) Who done this job?
(b) Who does this job?
(c) Who did this job?
(d) Who will do the job?

16. Can the door be broken by you?
(a) Can you break the door?
(b) Did you break the door?
(c) You can break the door?
(d) You broke the door?

17. Match the following.

List I (Active Voice)	List II (Passive Voice)
A. Your mom will forgive you.	1. You are being forgiven by your mom.
B. Your mom is forgiving you.	2. Why were we being scolded by her?
C. Why did she scold us?	3. You will be forgiven by your mom.
D. Why was she scolding us?	4. Why were we scolded by her?

Codes

	A	B	C	D		A	B	C	D
(a)	1	3	2	4	(b)	1	3	4	2
(c)	3	1	4	2	(d)	3	1	2	4

18. Choose the option that correctly changes the voice of the given sentence.
The boy gave the teacher flowers.

A. Flowers were given to the teacher by the boy.
B. Flowers were given to the boy by the teacher.
C. The boy was given flowers by the teacher.
D. The teacher was given flowers by the boy.

Codes
(a) Only A (b) B and C
(c) A and D (d) C and D

Direct and Indirect Speech

1 Mark Questions

Directions (Q. Nos. 1-5) Change the following into indirect speech.

1. Rohan said, "I will phone you tomorrow."
   (a) Rohan said that she will phone me the next day.
   (b) Rohan said that he would phone me the next day.
   (c) Rohan said that he would call me tomorrow.
   (d) Rohan said that he will phone me the next day.

2. "I love the Tom and Jerry show," Avni said.
   (a) Avni said that she loves the Tom and Jerry show.
   (b) Avni says that she loves the Tom and Jerry show.
   (c) Avni said that she loved the Tom and Jerry show.
   (d) Avni told that she loved the Tom and Jerry show.

3. Damini said to Kavita, "I work in a bank."
   (a) Damini said to Kavita that she works in a bank.
   (b) Damini said to Kavita that she worked in a bank.
   (c) Damini told to Kavita that she works in a bank.
   (d) Damini told Kavita that she worked in a bank.

4. Suman said, "The baby is sleeping."
   (a) Suman said that the baby has been sleeping.
   (b) Suman says that the baby was sleeping.
   (c) Suman says that the baby had been sleeping.
   (d) Suman said that the baby was sleeping.

5. Prisha said, "I enjoy working in my garden."
   (a) Prisha said that she enjoys working in my garden.
   (b) Prisha said that she enjoyed working in her garden.
   (c) Prisha says that she enjoyed working in her garden.
   (d) Prisha says that she enjoy working in her garden.

Directions (Q. Nos. 6-8) Complete the indirect/direct speech of the given sentences.

6. He said, "Hurrah! I won a prize."
   He .... that he had won a prize.
   (a) exclaimed with joy
   (b) said
   (c) exclaimed with sorrow
   (d) Told

7. He said that he was living in Paris.
   He said, "............"
   (a) I was living in Paris.
   (b) He was living in Paris.
   (c) He has been living in Paris.
   (d) I am living in Paris.

8. Madhur said, "I need help with my work."
   Madhur said that ....
   (a) he needs help with his work.
   (b) he needed help with my work.
   (c) I needed help with my work.
   (d) he needed help with his work.

Directions (Q. Nos. 9-12) Choose the correct direct form of the given sentences.

9. She asked me who I had seen.
   (a) She asked, "Who have you saw?"
   (b) She asked, "Who had you seen."
   (c) She asked, "Who did you saw?"
   (d) She asked, "Who did you see?"

10. Karan said that he travelled a lot in his job.
    (a) Karan said, "I travel a lot in my job."
    (b) Karan said, "I travelled a lot in my job."
    (c) Karan said, "I travel a lot."
    (d) Karan says, "I travel a lot in my job."

11. The boy said that he had hurt his leg.
    (a) The boy said, "Me have hurt my leg."
    (b) The boy said, "I have hurt my leg."
    (c) The boy said, "I have hurt leg."
    (d) The boy said, "I had hurt my leg."

12. The police warned us not to go in there.
    (a) The police said, "Don't go in."
    (b) The police said, "Don't go in now."
    (c) The police said, "Don't go in there."
    (d) The police said, "Don't go there."

2 Marks Questions

13. Match the following.

List I (Direct Speech)	List II (Indirect Speech)
A. She said, "I've missed my train."	1. Michael said that he would buy a new car.
B. Michael said, "I will buy a new car."	2. Mark said that Bill needed a pencil.
C. Mark said, "Bill needs a pencil."	3. The teacher asked if I had done my homework.
D. The teacher said, "Did you do your homework?"	4. She said that she had missed her train.

Codes

	A	B	C	D		A	B	C	D
(a)	4	1	2	3	(b)	1	4	3	2
(c)	3	2	4	1	(d)	2	3	1	4

Directions (Q. Nos. 14 and 15) Read the following sentences and choose which of them are in direct speech.

14. 1. He said, "I may buy a computer."
    2. He said, "If I won the lottery I would travel around the whole world."
    3. Shaina says that we should write our lessons carefully.

Codes
(a) Only 1   (b) Only 2
(c) 1 and 2   (d) 2 and 3

15. 1. Copernicus said, "The planets revolve around the sun."

2. The children said we wish we didn't have to take exams.

3. What did the teacher say, asked the student.

Codes

(a) Only 3   (b) 1 and 2

(c) 2 and 3   (d) Only 1

Directions (Q. Nos. 16 and 17) Read the following sentences and choose which of them are in indirect speech?

16. 1. Kabir asked if he might have a cup of tea.

2. He asked me what I wanted.

3. He told me that he could ski on that hill.

Codes

(a) 2 and 3   (b) 1 and 3

(c) Only 1   (d) All of these

17. 1. He said, "She will go there."

2. He told the stranger that he did not recognise him.

3. She said that "the patient had died in the hospital."

Codes

(a) Only 2

(b) 2 and 3

(c) 1 and 2

(d) None of the above

18. Match the following.

List-I (Direct Speech)		List-II (Indirect speech)
A.	The guard asked, "Who are you?"	1.	He exclaimed with sorrow that couldn't be that bad.
B.	She said, "Bring a glass of water, please."	2.	She ordered me to shut the door.
C.	She said, "Shut the door!"	3.	She requested me to bring a glass of water.
D.	"Alas! It can't be this bad." He said.	4.	The guard asked who I was.

Codes

	A	B	C	D			A	B	C	D
(a)	4	3	2	1	(b)		3	2	4	1
(c)	2	4	3	1	(d)		1	2	3	4

19. Read the conversation given below and complete the paragraph that follows.

Shopkeeper: What do you want to buy madam: brinjal, tomato, onion?

The Customer: One kilo of tomato and onion. Do you have carrots?

Shopkeeper: Sorry madam. No carrots. There are lots of radish.

The shopkeeper asked the customer ...(i)... The customer ...(ii)... She also asked him whether he has carrots. Shopkeeper replied ...(iii)...

(i) (a) if she wanted to buy brinjal, tomato or onion.

   (b) what she wanted to buy.

   (c) what she wants to buy.

   (d) what she wanted to buy.

(ii) (a) told him that she wanted one kilo tomato and onion.

   (b) said that she wanted one kilo of tomato and onion.

   (c) replied to him that she wants one kilo of tomato and onion.

   (d) told him that she wanted on kilo tomato and onion.

(iii) (a) that he had only radish.

   (b) that he had no carrots but he had lots of radish.

   (c) that he has no carrots but lots of radish.

   (d) that he has no carrots but lots of radish.

Chapter 14

Synonyms and Antonyms

1 Mark Questions

Directions (Q. Nos. 1-5) Find the suitable synonym for the underlined word in the given sentences.

1. It is very <u>difficult</u> to understand a foreign language.
   - (a) simple
   - (b) challenging
   - (c) normal
   - (d) easy

2. This toy is <u>inexpensive</u>.
   - (a) overpriced
   - (b) expensive
   - (c) cheap
   - (d) good

3. He never <u>reaches</u> on time.
   - (a) sees
   - (b) arrives
   - (c) does
   - (d) goes

4. Do you think I am <u>stupid</u>?
   - (a) foolish
   - (b) intelligent
   - (c) brilliant
   - (d) fast

5. He is a <u>fast</u> runner.
   - (a) slow
   - (b) energetic
   - (c) calm
   - (d) quick

Directions (Q. Nos. 6-9) In each of the following questions, select the option which is a synonym of the given word.

6. Weak
   - (a) Agile
   - (b) Frail
   - (c) Strong
   - (d) Hefty

7. Small
   - (a) Short
   - (b) Fine
   - (c) Tiny
   - (d) Flimsy

8. Alert
   - (a) Smart
   - (b) Watchful
   - (c) Rustic
   - (d) Live

9. Faith
   - (a) Proof
   - (b) Belief
   - (c) Repose
   - (d) Agree

Directions (Q. Nos. 10-13) Choose the suitable antonym for the underlined word in the given sentence.

10. The measurements were absolutely <u>accurate</u>.
    - (a) exact
    - (b) precise
    - (c) inexact
    - (d) correct

11. Silk does not <u>shrink</u> like other fabrics.
    - (a) bright
    - (b) expire
    - (c) expand
    - (d) excuse

12. Don't you think his account of things was <u>monotonous</u>?
    - (a) agreeable
    - (b) varied
    - (c) acceptable
    - (d) indecent

13. He has an <u>aversion</u> to milk.

(a) impression
(b) liking
(c) dislike
(d) ignorance

Directions (Q. Nos. 14-18) In each of the following questions, select the option which is an antonym of the given word.

14. Mean

(a) Happy   (b) Tall
(c) Weird   (d) Nice

15. Strong

(a) Thin   (b) Young
(c) Weak   (d) Light

16. Precise

(a) Brief   (b) Clear
(c) Vague   (d) Pretty

17. Agony

(a) Sympathy   (b) Suffering
(c) Pain   (d) Pleasure

18. Curtail

(a) Stop   (b) Cease
(c) Go   (d) Resume

2 Marks Questions

19. Match the words in List I with their antonyms given in List II.

List I		List II	
A.	Sweet	1.	Calm
B.	Windy	2.	Happy
C.	Scared	3.	Bitter
D.	Upset	4.	Confident

Codes

	A	B	C	D
(a)	2	1	3	4
(b)	3	2	1	4
(c)	3	1	4	2
(d)	4	3	1	2

20. In the question given below, List I consists of sentences with an underlined word. Match the underlined words with their antonyms.

List I		List II	
A.	Red light says, "<u>stop</u>".	1.	hatred
B.	Homework sometimes is very <u>boring</u>.	2.	unavailable
C.	The books are <u>available</u> at the school shop.	3.	go
D.	Children should be treated with <u>love</u>.	4.	interesting

Codes

	A	B	C	D		A	B	C	D
(a)	2	1	3	4	(b)	3	4	2	1
(c)	4	1	2	3	(d)	1	4	3	2

21. Match the words given in List I with their synonyms given in List II.

List I		List II	
A.	Deceptive	1.	Confinement
B.	Captivity	2.	Misleading
C.	Immerse	3.	Complicated
D.	Intricate	4.	Submerge

Codes

	A	B	C	D		A	B	C	D
(a)	2	1	3	4	(b)	4	3	2	1
(c)	2	1	4	3	(d)	4	3	1	2

22. Match the underlined words in List I with their synonyms in List II.

	List I	List II
A.	Divya's <u>arrival</u> brought complete silence to the room.	1. Join
B.	I hope this won't <u>occur</u> again.	2. Appearance
C.	The railway link would <u>connect</u> Kolkata to Delhi.	3. Lift
D.	Gradually <u>raise</u> your body into an upright position.	4. Happen

Codes

	A	B	C	D
(a)	3	2	4	1
(b)	1	3	2	4
(c)	2	4	1	3
(d)	4	1	3	2

23. Choose the option with the correct antonym(s) for 'create'.
A. Break, Demolish
B. Destroy, End, Wreck
C. Establish, Construct, Build
D. Dismantle, Form, Produce
Codes
(a) Only B
(b) A and B
(c) A, B and D
(d) Only C

24. Choose the option with the correct synonym(s) for 'permanent'.
A. Temporary
B. Changing, Short-term, Fleeting
C. Lasting, Enduring, Eternal
D. Fixed, Long-term, Changeless
Codes
(a) A and B
(b) Only B
(c) C and D
(d) Only C

25. Choose the option with the correct pair of antonyms.
(a) Infant-Baby, Give-Offer, Brief-Long
(b) Borrow-Lend, Believe-Trust, Give-Offer
(c) Gain-Lose, Deep-Shallow, Give-Offer
(d) Borrow-Lend, Deep-Shallow, Gain-Lose, Brief-Long

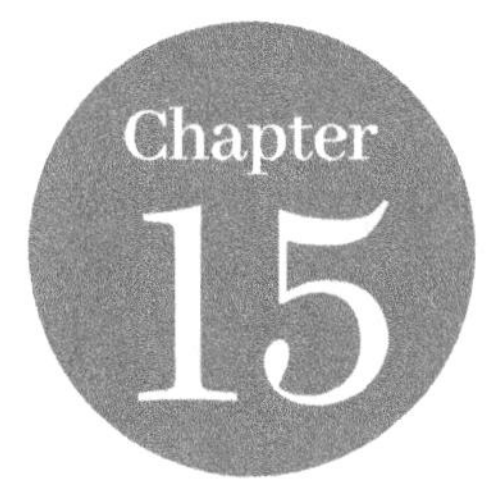

Chapter 15

Homophones and Homonyms

1 Mark Questions

Directions (Q. Nos. 1-10) Fill in the blanks with the correct homophones given in the options.

1. By the time we went .... the store was closed.
   (a) their   (b) there
   (c) Both (a) and (b)   (d) Neither (a) nor (b)

2. I wish you .... turn down the loud music.
   (a) would   (b) wood
   (c) wooed   (d) None of these

3. The lion kept an eye on his ....
   (a) prey   (b) pray
   (c) Both (a) and (b)   (d) None of these

4. The monkey wanted to break off the .... to eat it.
   (a) pair   (b) pare
   (c) pear   (d) peer

5. When are you going .... the party?
   (a) two   (b) too
   (c) to   (d) None of these

6. Saksham was .... in supporting the protesting farmers.
   (a) write   (b) rite
   (c) right   (d) Both (b) and (c)

7. You should not .... the law.
   (a) brake   (b) break
   (c) Both (a) and (b)   (d) None of these

8. She sometime puts nail varnish on her .... nails.
   (a) to   (b) too
   (c) tow   (d) toe

9. I liked the actress's distinctive ....
   (a) gate   (b) gait
   (c) get   (d) Both (b) and (c)

10. Did you .... the potatoes, Shama?
    (a) peal   (b) peel
    (c) Both (a) and (b)   (d) None of these

Directions (Q. Nos. 11-15) Choose the sentence with the incorrect usage of underlined homonyms.

11. (a) Komuro formed a <u>rock</u> band with some friends while in college.
    (b) I will <u>rock</u> you hard if you don't listen to me.
    (c) To build the tunnel, they had to cut through 500 feet of solid <u>rock</u>.
    (d) Don't worry about your performance, you will <u>rock</u> it.

12. (a) You cannot <u>mean</u> the way I want.

(b) What does this sentence <u>mean</u>?

(c) He has to calculate the <u>mean</u> of these figures.

(d) Manya is such a <u>mean</u> person that nobody wants to talk to her.

13. (a) If you suspect a gas leak do not strike a <u>match</u> or use electricity.

(b) We do not <u>match</u> to strike a fire.

(c) Her fingerprints <u>match</u> those found at the scene of the crime.

(d) Shikha and Tapan make a perfect <u>match</u>.

14. (a) The <u>band</u> was playing old Beatles songs.

(b) She always ties her hair in a <u>band</u>.

(c) Many insects are <u>banned</u> black and yellow.

(d) The black and white <u>bands</u> on road depict zebra crossing.

15. (a) You cannot <u>spring</u> me up.

(b) I'm sorry to <u>spring</u> it on you, but I've been offered another job.

(c) He was born in the <u>spring</u> of 1944.

(d) The couch and the mattress have lost their <u>springs</u>.

16. Choose the word that can fill the blanks in both sentences.

Dad said I could ……… this page from the newspaper.
I knew Himani was sad when I saw a ……… in her eye.

(a) clip   (b) copy

(c) gleam   (d) tear

17. Which of the following is not a homophone pair?

(a) Floor-Flour

(b) Few-Phew

(c) Gilt-Guilt

(d) Cent-Saint

2 Marks Questions

Directions (Q. Nos. 18-20) Choose the sentences with the incorrect use of underlined word i.e. homonyms.

18. A. The rabbits were kept in a <u>pen</u>.

B. She cleaned the floor with a <u>pen</u>.

C. Use a blue <u>pen</u> to sign this document.

D. Samir kept the <u>pen</u> at the back part of his house.

Codes

(a) A and B

(b) Only B

(c) C and D

(d) Only D

19. A. <u>Show</u> me that paper, please.

B. The <u>show</u> began at 10 a.m.

C. Kavya wanted to give me a <u>show</u>.

D. Young girls are lured by the charm of the <u>show</u> business industry.

Codes

(a) A and B   (b) Only D

(c) Only C   (d) C and D

20. A. Satyajit's movies were <u>hailed</u> by the audience.

B. Nutan <u>hailed</u> a passer-by to seek help.

C. It was <u>hailing</u> today morning.

D. Do you <u>hail</u> nearby?

Codes

(a) Only A   (b) A and B

(c) Only C   (d) Only D

Directions (Q. Nos. 21 and 22) Choose the sentences with the correct usage of the underlined words i.e. homophones.

21. A. If you mix <u>blue</u> and yellow, you get green.

B. The bomb <u>blue</u> a huge hole in the ground.

C. A sudden gust of wind <u>blew</u> the door shut.

D. She handed him a light <u>blew</u> shirt to match with his tie.

Codes

(a) A and D

(b) B and C

(c) A and C

(d) B and D

22. A. She <u>kneaded</u> the dought and left it to rise.

B. My bicycle had a puncture and <u>needed</u> patching up.

C. Drastic measures are <u>kneaded</u> to clean up the mess.

D. She nodded and <u>kneaded</u> her temples with her fingertips.

Codes

(a) A and B   (b) Only D

(c) Only D   (d) A, B and D

23. Choose the word which will fill all the three blanks appropriately.

I was .... to train him. She finally .... her application for the job. I .... Helen away and sat down.

(a) sent

(b) scent

(c) cent

(d) All of the above

24. Choose the word from the options that can fill the blanks in all three sentences given below.

A. Was that .... his father got all that money?

B. .... did you plan to sleep tonight?

C. Do you know .... the fountain is?

(a) ware   (b) where

(c) wear   (d) Both (b) and (c)

25. Match the following homophones given in List I with their meanings given in List II.

List I		List II
A. Too	1.	To draw or pull along behind
B. To	2.	Any of the five separate parts at the end of the foot
C. Tow	3.	Also
D. Toe	4.	Expressing motion in the direction of a location

Codes

	A	B	C	D		A	B	C	D
(a)	1	4	2	3	(b)	2	3	4	1
(c)	3	4	1	2	(d)	4	2	1	3

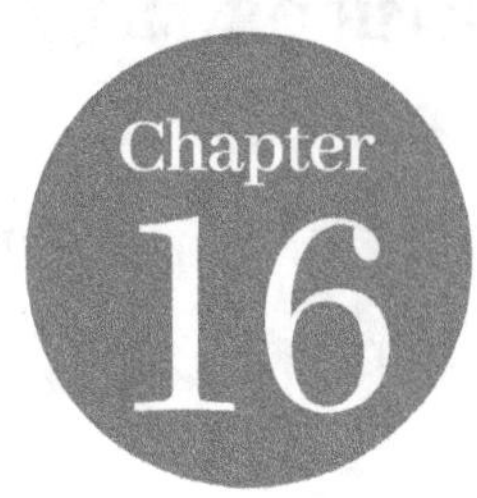

One Word Substitution

Directions (Q. Nos. 1-7) Choose the correct one word substitution for the following.

1. One who foretells events.

   (a) Astronaut   (b) Astrologer
   (b) Autocrat   (d) Democrat

2. One who entertains a guest.

   (a) Audience   (b) Host
   (c) Spectator   (d) Courier

3. A woman whose husband is dead.

   (a) Widow   (b) Widower
   (c) Spinster   (d) Dame

4. Someone who is excessively in love with himself.

   (a) Insolvent   (b) Numismatist
   (c) Lunatic   (d) Narcissist

5. An examination of a dead body to determine the cause of death.

   (a) Suicide
   (b) Alchemy
   (c) Postmortem
   (d) Postdoctoral

6. A person who writes beautiful writing.

   (a) Cartographer
   (b) Compere
   (c) Astronaut
   (d) Calligrapher

7. A keeper or custodian of a museum or other collection.

   (a) Traitor   (b) Florist
   (c) Anchor   (d) Curator

Directions (Q. Nos. 8-11) Choose the correct meaning of the following one word substitutions.

8. Garage

   (a) A place for housing furniture
   (b) A place for keeping clothes
   (c) A place for storing pictures
   (d) A place for housing cars

9. Drey

   (a) Nest of a rabbit   (b) Nest of a squirrel
   (c) Nest of an eagle   (d) Nest of an owl

10. Morgue

   (a) A place where specimen of plants are kept
   (b) A place where important documents are kept
   (c) A place where dead bodies are kept for identification
   (d) A place where grain is kept

11. Cartographer

   (a) A person who takes pictures from space
   (b) A person who makes maps

(c) A person who makes drawing of buildings

(d) A person who writes essays

Directions (Q. Nos. 12 and 13) Match the one words given in List I with their description given in List II.

12.

List I		List II
A. Pilgrim	1.	The property left to someone by a will
B. Legacy	2.	A man whose wife is dead
C. Introvert	3.	One who journeys to a holy place
D. Widower	4.	One who does not express himself/herself freely

Codes

	A	B	C	D
(a)	3	1	4	2
(b)	2	3	4	1
(c)	1	4	2	3
(d)	4	2	3	1

13.

List I		List II
A. Epidemic	1.	A disease affecting many persons at the same place and time
B. Elocution	2.	Absence of rain for a long time
C. Drought	3.	One who reports news or conducts interviews for the newspaper or broadcasting media or press
D. Reporter	4.	The art of effective speaking or oral reading

Codes

	A	B	C	D		A	B	C	D
(a)	3	2	4	1	(b)	2	3	4	1
(c)	1	4	2	3	(d)	4	2	3	1

Directions (Q. Nos. 14 and 16) Choose the correct statements.

14. A. Amphibian: A cold-blooded vertebrate animal that is born in water and breathes with gills.

B. Chronometer: The arrangement of events or dates in the order of their occurrence.

C. Ephemeral: Lasting for a very short time.

D. Souvenir: A thing that is kept as a reminder of a person, place, or event.

Codes

(a) A, B and C

(b) B, C and D

(c) A, C and D

(d) All of the above

15. A. Democracy: A form of government with a monarch at the head.

B. Apiary: A large cage, building, or enclosure to keep birds.

C. Cemetery: A large burial ground, especially one not in a churchyard.

D. Hangar: A large building with an extensive floor area, typically for housing aircrafts.

Codes

(a) A and B   (b) B and D

(c) B and C   (d) C and D

16. A. Orchard: A piece of enclosed land planted with fruit trees.

B. Tannery: A place where animal hides are tanned.

C. Ascetic: One who leads a simple life.

D. Emigrant: Someone who leaves one country to settle in another.

(a) A and C   (b) Only D

(c) B and D   (d) All of these

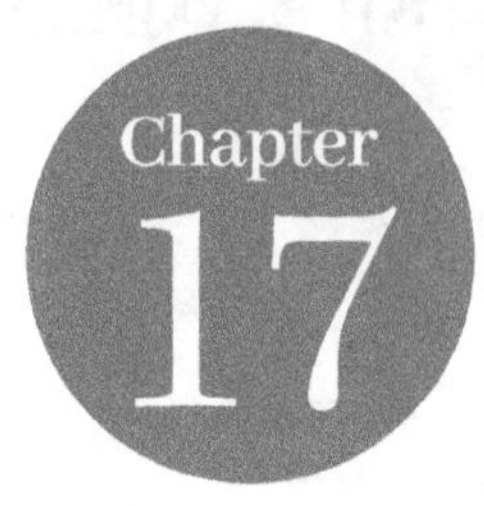

Chapter 17

Idioms and Phrases

1 Mark Questions

Directions (Q. Nos. 1-5) Select the most appropriate meaning of the given idioms/phases.

1. In a pickle
   - (a) In jubiliation
   - (b) In deep sorrow
   - (c) In trouble
   - (d) In great pain

2. Red letter day
   - (a) A very hot day
   - (b) A frightful day
   - (c) A very special day
   - (d) A very cold day

3. Out of sorts
   - (a) To be slightly unwell
   - (b) To discuss private matters in public
   - (c) To continue to complain
   - (d) To go outside

4. Throw in the towel
   - (a) Drop something
   - (b) Face the situation
   - (c) Think of a solution
   - (d) Admit defeat

5. As the crow flies
   - (a) To be directionless
   - (b) To be uncertain
   - (c) A long winding path
   - (d) The shortest route

Directions (Q. Nos. 6-10) For each of the following sentences four alternatives are given. Choose the correct meaning of the idioms given in bold.

6. Sumit had to **look high and low** before he could get his scooter key.
   - (a) look nowhere
   - (b) look down
   - (c) look everywhere
   - (d) look up

7. At any outing, Ruchika is always **in high spirits**.
   - (a) talkative
   - (b) cheerful
   - (c) drunk
   - (d) uncontrollable

8. She rejected his proposal for marriage **point blank**.
   - (a) directly
   - (b) pointedly
   - (c) briefly
   - (d) indirectly

9. We should be cautious of our **green-eyed** friends.
   - (a) rich
   - (b) handsome
   - (c) enthusiastic
   - (d) jealous

10. Being recognised at public places is a **part and parcel** of an actor's life.
   - (a) avoidable thing
   - (b) unavoidable thing
   - (c) great thing
   - (d) dull thing

Directions (Q. Nos. 11-15) Complete the idioms/phrases by filling up the blanks.

11. Eat like a ....
(a) beggar   (b) swan
(c) dog   (d) bird

12. A .... republic
(a) mango
(b) diamond
(c) banana
(d) pear

13. Call it ....
(a) a month   (b) a year
(c) a day   (d) a week

14. .... the pump
(a) Privy   (b) Prime
(c) Repair   (d) Take

15. A bone of ....
(a) retention   (b) contention
(c) detention   (d) attention

2 Marks Questions

16. Complete the Idioms/Phrases by matching items in List I with List II

List I		List II	
A.	blue-eyed	1.	pie order
B.	in apple	2.	boy
C.	slip of	3.	tied
D.	be tongue	4.	the tongue

Codes

	A	B	C	D		A	B	C	D
(a)	2	1	3	4	(b)	2	1	4	3
(c)	1	3	4	2	(d)	4	3	2	1

17. Match the idioms given in List I with their meanings given in List II.

List I		List II	
A.	On the ball	1.	To die
B.	Kick the bucket	2.	Confused
C.	Bolt from the blue	3.	Doing a good job
D.	At sea	4.	A complete surprise

Codes

	A	B	C	D		A	B	C	D
(a)	3	1	4	2	(b)	2	3	1	4
(c)	3	4	1	2	(d)	4	3	2	1

18. Which of the following sentences use the underlined idiom correctly?

A. He wishes to <u>get rid of</u> depression.

B. He will be with you <u>through thick and thin</u>.

C. Cindy was <u>swept under the rug</u> when she stood first in the class.

D. It was quite a <u>green thumb</u>, but my father managed to avoid hitting the animal that ran across the highway.

Codes
(a) A and D
(b) Only C
(c) A and B
(d) B, C and D

19. Consider the following sentences.

1. The idiom 'once in a blue moon' means 'something that happens very rarely'.

2. The idiom 'bite your tongue' means 'to talk for a long time'.

3. The idiom 'spill the beans' means 'to reveal a secret'.

Which of these sentences are correct?
(a) 1 and 2
(b) 1 and 3
(c) 2 and 3
(d) All of the above

20. Match the underlined idioms given in the sentences in List I with their meanings in List II.

List I	List II
A. <u>Out</u> of <u>the blue</u>, a deer came in front of my car.	1. Out of control
B. When the police arrived, they realised the party was getting <u>out of hand</u>.	2. Fix the standards acceptable for the task
C. We would better pack the car and <u>hit the road</u> before it gets dark.	3. Out of nowhere or unexpectedly
D. Don't <u>set the bar</u> so high that it becomes impossible to achieve anything.	4. To depart

Codes

	A	B	C	D			A	B	C	D
(a)	1	3	4	2		(b)	3	1	4	2
(c)	4	3	2	1		(d)	2	1	3	4

21. Match the following.

List I (Idioms and Phrases)	List II (Meaning)
A. Bated breath	1. anxiety and expectancy
B. Rise to the occasion	2. to act as the occasion demands
C. Wear and Tear	3. damage caused by use
D. At odds	4. In dispute

Codes

	A	B	C	D			A	B	C	D
(a)	3	4	1	2		(b)	4	2	3	1
(c)	1	2	3	4		(d)	2	4	1	3

22. Match the following.

List I (Idioms and Phrases)	List II (Meaning)
A. Assume airs	1. Pretty and expensive but not useful
B. In a flutter	2. an unreliable and deceitful person
C. White expensive	3. to pretend superiority
D. A snake in the grass	4. excited

Codes

	A	B	C	D			A	B	C	D
(a)	3	4	1	2		(b)	4	2	3	1
(c)	2	1	3	4		(d)	2	4	1	3

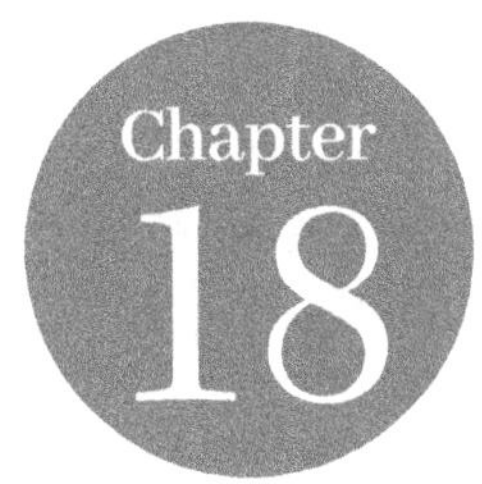

Chapter 18

Jumbled Words and Sentences

1 Mark Questions

Directions (Q. Nos. 1-6) Rearrange the following letters to form meaningful words.

1. drrhioea
   (a) Diarrheoa   (b) Diaorrhea
   (c) Diarrohea   (d) Diarrhoea

2. lllauby
   (a) llulaby   (b) Lalluby
   (c) Lullaby   (d) Llaluby

3. gearouc
   (a) Courage   (b) Ragecou
   (c) Gaeruco   (d) Cuorega

4. ncesiec
   (a) Niececs   (b) Sceinec
   (c) Scemce   (d) Science

5. sferaels
   (a) Fareless   (b) Faerless
   (c) Fearless   (d) Feraless

6. rewolfnus
   (a) sunflower   (b) Funslower
   (c) Runsflow   (d) None of these

Directions (Q. Nos. 9-12) Rearrange the words to form meaningful sentences.

9. beautifully/shone/the/so/sun
   (a) The shone sun so beautifully.
   (b) The sun shone so beautifully.
   (c) The sun beautifully shone so.
   (d) The shone so beautifully sun.

10. have / hours / three / been / studying / for / we
   (a) Three hours been have studying for.
   (b) We have been studying for three hours.
   (c) We been have studying for three hours.
   (d) Three hours have been for studying we.

11. morning / do/ every / what / you/ do/?
   (a) What do you every morning?
   (b) Do you do what every morning?
   (c) What do you do every morning?
   (d) Every morning what do you?

12. how /their task / long / been / doing / have / they?
   (a) How they have been long doing?
   (b) How long have they doing the task?
   (c) How long have they been doing their task?
   (d) How long the task have been doing they the task?

2 Marks Questions

Directions (Q. Nos. 13-15) In the questions given below, there is a sentence with jumbled up parts. Rearrange these parts, which are labelled A, B, C and D to produce the correct sentence. Choose the proper sequence.

13. A. I wanted to tell her
B. not to talk to him
C. not listen to me.
D. but she would

Codes

(a) ABCD   (b) ABDC

(c) ADBC   (d) BCAD

14. A. She wondered if
B. work hard for a living
C. he would ever
D. because he was so rich.

Codes

(a) ACBD   (b) ABCD

(c) ABDC   (d) BCDA

15. A. I was certain
B. the management meeting.
C. be allowed to attend
D. that subordinates would not

Codes

(a) ABCD   (b) ABDC

(c) ADCB   (d) BCDA

Directions (Q. Nos. 16 and 17) In the sentence given below, there is a incomplete sentence with jubled up parts. Rearrange these parts, which are labelled A, B, C and D to produce the correct sentence. Choose the proper sequence.

16. A classical Chinese painting….
A. as would a
B. is not meant to
C. Western figurative painting
D. represent an actual view

Codes

(a) ACBD   (b) BDAC

(c) BACD   (d) DCAB

17. Once reluctant to be …….
A. seems to have
B. Congress Vice President Rahul Gandhi
C. seen with Lalu Yadav
D. turned the page

Codes

(a) DCAB   (b) CBAD

(c) ADCB   (d) DCBA

Directions (Q. Nos. 18 and 19) Rearrange the following sentence into meaningful paragraph.

18. A. In his literacy work he spoke of human life which mere intellect does not speak.
B. He has also given innocent joy to many children by his stories like 'Kabuliwalah'.
C. These songs are sung not only in Bengal but all over the country.
D. Rabindranath's great works sprang from intensity of vision and feelings.
E. He sang of beauty and heroism, nobility and charm.

Codes

(a) BAEDC   (b) CDEBA

(c) DABEC   (d) CBEAD

19. A. If they are dissatisfied, they have a cause to complain.
B. Rather they are an embodiment of patience.
C. Teachers ought to set an example.
D. Yet they should exercise restraint.
E. Patience is one of the greatest virtues.

Codes

(a) CBADE   (b) EDCBA

(c) ABCDE   (d) CADBE

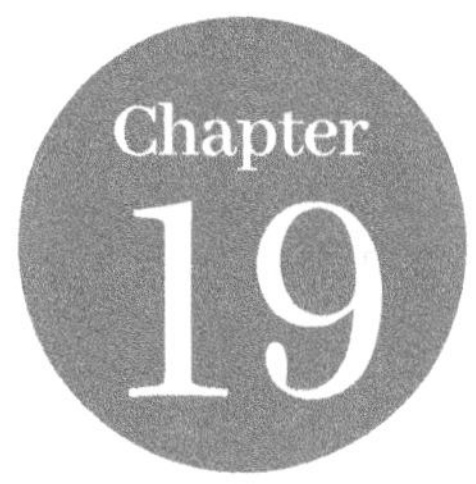# Spelling Test

1 Mark Questions

Directions (Q. Nos. 1-15) Select the correctly spelt words from the following.

1. (a) Cheif   (b) Chief
   (c) Cheef   (d) Cheaf

2. (a) Heape   (b) Heep
   (c) Haep   (d) Heap

3. (a) Batallion   (b) Batalion
   (c) Battallion   (d) Battalion

4. (a) Receipt   (b) Reciept
   (c) Receept   (d) Reaceipt

5. (a) Acheivement   (b) Acheevment
   (c) Achievement   (d) Acheavement

6. (a) Knowledge   (b) Knoledge
   (c) Knoelege   (d) Knoeledge

7. (a) Succed
   (b) Succeede
   (c) Suckceed
   (d) Succeed

8. (a) Propegate   (b) Propogete
   (c) Propogait   (d) Propogate

9. (a) Psychosocal   (b) Psychosocial
   (c) Psykosocial   (d) Sychosocial

10. (a) Soverignty   (b) Sovereignty
    (c) Sovereignity   (d) Sowereignty

11. (a) Calculus   (b) Calkulus
    (c) Somber   (d) Stoik

12. (a) Plomp   (b) Fraued
    (c) Pneumonia   (d) Fiegn

13. (a) Business   (b) Comendable
    (c) Admmisible   (d) Celuloid

14. (a) Exammination   (b) Litegation
    (c) Kalcification   (d) Summation

15. (a) Vaccinee   (b) Sanetize
    (c) Jaib   (d) Quarantine

2 Marks Questions

Directions (Q. Nos. 16-20) Fill in the blanks by choosing the correctly spelt word from the given options.

16. The tyre of my scooty got .... today.
    (a) punktured   (b) punctured
    (c) puncturred   (d) punctared

17. I .... dropped the vase.
    (a) accidentaly   (b) accidentalli
    (c) acidentally   (d) accidentally

18. The students had to fill up a .... before joining the online lecture.
    (a) questionaire   (b) questionare
    (c) questionnaire   (d) questionniare

19. What is the most .... moment of your life?
    (a) emmbarrassing   (b) embarrasseng
    (c) embarrassing   (d) embairrassing

20. My father was given a government .... in Delhi Cantt.
   - (a) accomodation
   - (b) accommodation
   - (c) accammodation
   - (d) accemodation

Directions (Q. Nos 21-32) Select the incorrectly spelt words from the following.

21. (a) Pessimistic   (b) Separate
   (c) Regent   (d) Comprihension

22. (a) Proffesional   (b) Privilege
   (c) Appearance   (d) Attendance

23. (a) Agitation   (b) Repeal
   (c) Repel   (d) Grammer

24. (a) Philosophy
   (b) Society
   (c) Calamity
   (d) Assurence

25. (a) Gospel   (b) Solemn
   (c) Barbar   (d) Cobbler

26. (a) Descendant   (b) Enmity
   (c) Profecient   (d) Impression

27. (a) Licence   (b) Procedure
   (c) Vacuum   (d) Reputted

28. (a) Potable   (b) Solvable
   (c) Manageble   (d) Movable

29. (a) Carrying   (b) Benefitted
   (c) Murmured   (d) Decieve

30. (a) Pedestrien   (b) Sophisticated
   (c) Encoding   (d) Surrogate

31. (a) Schedule   (b) Vaccum
   (c) Tranquility   (d) Acceleration

32. (a) Bllade   (b) Commander
   (c) Decathalon   (d) Analysis

Reading Comprehension

1 Mark Questions

Directions (Q. Nos. 1-5) Read the passages carefully and answer the questions that follow.

Passage I

To the children, the park seemed to be shrinking. Cass could remember when the paddock at the bottom of the valley had been full of bushes and long yellow grass. Great for playing hidey in. Now, it was gone.

First came the two high squat blocks of units that hide the early winter Sun. Within an year, what was left of the tall grass was covered by identical red brick town houses. The paddock had disappeared.

Trumper Park was their island in the middle of the city noise. The Trumper tree grew in the centre of the park half-way up the hill, its great grey branches spreading wide, its leaves changing from olive-green to yellow-gold as the year grew older.

Mrs Valchase hated that tree. Its leaves blew into her walled garden. The fruit bats that made it their home were much too noisy. And now she'd applied to the council to have it cut down.

The Becketts and their neighbours had formed a residents' committee to save the tree, but their negotiations with the overbearing Mrs Valchase had failed. She insisted the tree be cut down. 'It blocks my view,' she claimed.

The grass looked green and inviting under the Trumper Tree. Cass threw herself down in the shade, stretching her arms and legs on the cool grass. Lying like this, she gazed into the spreading canopy of branches. Dark green leaves patchworked with blue sky drifted and changed with the breeze, dappled sunlight flecking the ancient grey roots. 'It really is a special tree. Mum's right, it does seem to know everything.'

'You talk as if the tree is a person, Cass.' Carl bit into a sandwich and Cass stretched out her hand for one.

'I suppose I do a bit. But I can't imagine it not being there. What are we going to do? We must do something.'

Carl sat chewing, his glasses balanced on the very tip of his nose. One more chew and they would slip off. 'Well', Carl lifted his head and his glasses slid back into place, 'I don't know if we can do anything more, Cass. If adults can't stop them, what can we do?'

1. 'The park seemed to be shrinking'. Why did the children feel or say this?

   (a) The park was overcrowded.

   (b) Part of the park was occupied.

   (c) The park was gradually being replaced by buildings.

   (d) The favourite tree of the children was being cut down.

2. 'Trumper Park was their island in the middle of the city noise'. This means that the park ....

   (a) occupied a central location in the city.

   (b) was situated at the noisiest part of the city.

   (c) had a paddock to relax.

   (d) was a much desired place away from the noise of the city.

3. Which word in the 5th paragraph supports the view that Mrs Valchase is overbearing?

   (a) failed   (b) insisted

   (c) claimed   (d) blocks

4. The word 'canopy' in the 6th paragraph would mean ....

   (a) umbrella   (b) covering

   (c) floor   (d) jungle

5. An antonym of the word 'spreading' used in the 3rd paragraph is

   (a) smudging   (b) restricting

   (c) moving   (d) streaking

Passage II

Directions (Q. Nos. 6-10) Read the passage carefully and answer the questions that follow.

A tornado is a tight, funnel-shaped column of spinning air. The speed of spin increases as its diameter narrows. Within the funnel, air pressure is so low that the difference in pressure inside the funnel and outside it can make a building <u>explode</u> if a tornado passes over it.

Tornadoes are amazing as much as they are terrifying. A tornado can rip trees out by their roots, derail trains and sweep people, animals and even small buildings into the air. But, particularly in the case of people and animals, the tornado can land them back safely on Earth and completely unharmed. On 29th May, 1986, 12 school children were sucked up by a tornado in Western China. They were found on some sand dunes some 20 km away after the tornado had passed, perfectly safe.

A tornado can create much damage but the area it wrecks is quite small. The path of greatest destruction thus far recorded is slightly more than 100 metres wide. Because of this fact, a tornado can cause total destruction to a house on one side of a street while leaving a house on the opposite side untouched.

It is difficult to measure the exact speed of wind in the centre of a tornado as monitoring equipment can never survive the <u>onslaught</u>. It has been estimated that the speed of wind there is about 400 km/h. Whatever it is, a consolation is that tornadoes are short-lived and die out usually within an hour or two.

6. Spinning air inside a tornado increases its speed when ....

   (a) the funnel's diameter expands

   (b) the air pressure reduces

   (c) the funnel's diameter decreases

   (d) the air pressure of outside and inside becomes equal

7. How can tornadoes be amazing? It can be when ....

(a) it causes millions of deaths

(b) it leaves much debris on Earth

(c) it causes much destruction

(d) it can bring back man and animals on Earth safe and unharmed.

8. The tornado may cause a building to explode because of ....

(a) its strength

(b) difference in air pressure between its inside and outside

(c) its duration

(d) the force in its column of spinning air

9. A synonym of the word 'explode' as used in 1st paragraph is ....

(a) rage   (b) escalate

(c) burst   (d) ridicule

10. The word 'onslaught' in the last paragraph would mean ....

(a) a large number of people or things

(b) assault

(c) retreat

(d) charge

2 Marks Questions

Passage III

Directions (Q. Nos. 11-14) Read the passage carefully and answer the questions that follow.

Butterflies are some of the most interesting insects on the planet Earth. There are more than seventeen thousand different kinds of butterflies! Butterflies come in all shapes and sizes.

Butterflies go through four main stages of life. The first stage is the egg stage, followed by the larva stage. As a larva, or caterpillar, the future butterfly eats as much as possible. As it grows, it sheds its outer skin, or exoskeleton. This may happen four or five times. After a few weeks, the caterpillar enters the next stage of its life, the chrysalis stage.

In the chrysalis, the caterpillar will liquify into a soup of living cells. Then, it will reorganise into a butterfly and the metamorphosis is complete. In later parts of the chrysalis stage, you can see the forming butterfly through the chrysalis.

When the butterfly emerges from the chrysalis, it pumps its wings to send blood through them so that it can fly. Most butterflies only live a couple of weeks, just enough time to drink flower nectar and to mate. Some, like the Monarch butterfly, however, may live many months.

11. Which of the following is not TRUE?

(a) Butterflies must wait until blood drains into their wings before flying.

(b) The butterfly may shed its skin 10 to 12 times.

(c) Caterpillars liquify into a soup of living cells.

(d) Most butterflies live for weeks, at the most for a few months.

12. The second stage of life of a butterfly is ....

(a) larva   (b) egg

(c) chrysalis   (d) butterfly

13. The word 'metamorphosis' used in 2nd paragraph of the passage would mean ....

(a) translation   (b) transformation

(c) stagnation   (d) adjustment

14. Find the antonym of the word 'emerges' given in the last paragraph.

(a) appears   (b) reveals

(c) disappears   (d) rises

Poem

Directions (Q. Nos. 15-19) Read the following poem carefully and answer the questions that follow.

The sun descending in the west,

The evening star does shine;

The birds are silent in their nest,

And I must seek for mine.

     The moon, like a flower,

     In heaven's high bower,

     With silent delight

     Sits and smiles on the night.

Farewell, green fields and happy groves,

Where flocks have took delight:

Where lambs have <u>nibbled</u>, silent moves

The feet of angels bright;

     Unseen they pour blessing,

     And joy without ceasing,

     On each bud and blossom,

     And each sleeping bosom.

They look in every <u>thoughtless</u> nest,

Where birds are covered warm;

They visit caves of every beast,

To keep them all from harm.

     If they see any weeping

     That should have been sleeping,

     They pour sleep on their head,

     And sit down by their bed.

15. The evening star rises when ....

(a) the birds leave their nests

(b) it is midnight

(c) it is dawn

(d) the sun descends in the west

16. The poet compares Moon to ....

(a) a flower

(b) a bird in the nest

(c) an evening star

(d) an angel

17. In this poem, 'bower' represents ....

(a) a potted plant

(b) a framework that supports climbing plants

(c) a bouquet of flowers

(d) a flower vase

18. The meaning of the word 'nibbled' used in the 3rd stanza of the poem is ....

(a) eaten a small quantity

(b) taken a small bite

(c) taken a mouthful

(d) tasted

19. The nest is described as 'thoughtless' because ....

(a) the angels are blessing the birds to be happy

(b) the birds are covered in the warmth of their nest

(c) it is made without any thought

(d) the occupants are asleep without any worry

Writing Skills

1 Mark Questions

Directions (Q.Nos. 1-5) Format of a notice is given below in which different parts are numbered. Identify the numbers by choosing the correct option.

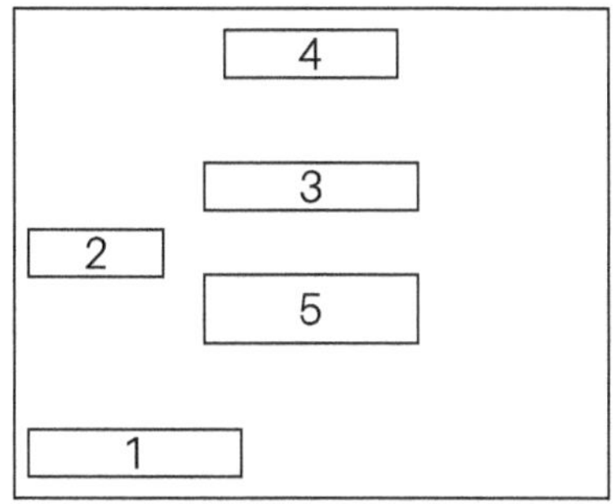

1. The item identified as **1** is ....
   (a) heading
   (b) notice
   (c) designation of the issuer
   (d) date

2. The item identified as **2** is ....
   (a) name of the organisation
   (b) subject of the notice
   (c) subject matter of the notice
   (d) date of the notice

3. The item identified as **3** is ....
   (a) subject of the notice
   (b) name of the issuing organisation
   (c) the word 'Notice'
   (d) date of the notice

4. The item identified as **4** is ....
   (a) designation of the issuer of the notice
   (b) name of the institution /organisation
   (c) subject of the notice
   (d) date of the notice

5. The item identified as **5** is ....
   (a) date of the notice
   (b) contents of the notice
   (c) subject of the notice
   (d) issuer's signature

Directions (Q. Nos. 6-8) A message is given below in which different parts are numbered. Identify the number by choosing the correct option.

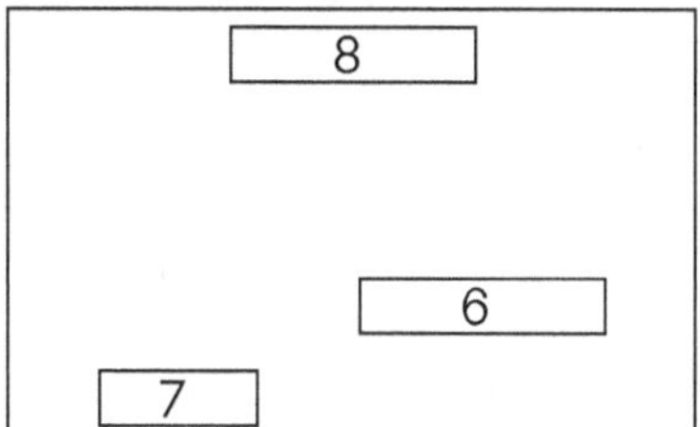

6. The item identified as **6** is ....
   (a) the word 'Message'
   (b) content
   (c) name of the writer
   (d) date

7. The item identified as **7** is ....

 (a) date of the message
 (b) the word 'message'
 (c) subject matter of the message
 (d) name of the person who has written the message

8. The item identified as **8** is ....

 (a) the content
 (b) name of person the message is written to
 (c) the word 'Message'
 (d) date of message

Directions (Q. Nos. 9-14) Read the story carefully and answer the questions that follow.

There was an old man living in a village. He had four sons and they were very lazy. The old man fell sick and was ....(9)....... his last days in bed. He worried a lot about his sons' future as the young men hesitated to work. The sons believed that luck would favour them.

The old man's health deteriorated day by day and he decided to talk to his sons about their future. However, his sons did not listen to him. The old man ......(10)...... to let his sons realise the importance of work.

He called all his sons and let them sit near him on his bed. He said he had a treasure box with gold coins and expensive gems for them and wanted to share the treasure equally among them so that they could lead a happy, prosperous life. The young men were very happy and asked where their father had placed the ......(11)...... . The old man replied, 'I cannot exactly remember the place where I had hidden the treasure from the others. However, the treasure box is buried in our land. I'm really not sure about the place where I had .....(12).....'.

Even though the lazy young sons were happy, they were sad that the old man forgot the place where the treasure was hidden. After a few days, the old man died. The sons decided ......(13)...... to find the treasure box.

After sometime, they realised that it was the hard work that was mentioned as 'Treasure Box' by their father. They forgot their laziness, and worked hard, earned money and lived happily.

9. (a) nearing (b) approaching
 (c) counting (d) measuring

10. (a) played a game
 (b) played a tune
 (c) played music
 (d) played a trick

11. (a) money (b) treasure
 (c) coins   (d) gems

12. (a) lost the treasure box
 (b) covered the treasure box
 (c) hidden the treasure box
 (d) wrapped the treasure box

13. (a) to uncover the land
 (b) to dig the land
 (c) to locate the land
 (d) look for the land

14. What can be a suitable title of this story?
 (a) Old man and his lazy sons
 (b) The treasure box
 (c) Hard work is the best treasure
 (d) Lazy boys and the treasure box

Directions (Q. Nos. 15-17) An informal letter is given below. Complete it by filling the blanks.

17 LIC Apartments

Lucknow -226001

.......**(15)**.......

Dear Jazzy,

Many thanks for your letter and photographs. They brought back very happy memories of our holiday. Indeed the time spent ....**(16)**....... has ended up being one of the best I have had so far. India is full of fascinating places and your company was really wonderful. In future more such ....**(17)**....... should be planned. Do let me know when you are planning to visit my place. What a joy it would be to see you and have you amongst us.

Catch you later

Michael

15. (a) Pincode (b) Time
    (c) Name of state (d) 3rd July, 20xx

16. (a) with you (b) alone
    (c) together (d) family

17. (a) outings (b) trips
    (c) picnics (d) meetings

2 Marks Questions

Directions (Q. Nos. 18-20) A formal letter is given below. Complete it by filling in the blanks.

To

The Principal

XYZ School

Delhi-90

    Subject ....**(18)**.......

Respected Madam,

I am Muskan Gupta, a student of class X-C at your school. With all due respect, I would like to bring to your notice that the nature of my father's job is not static as he is an army personnel. His transfer is due on the 2nd of the upcoming month.

Hereby, I request you to grant my School Leaving Certificate so that I can ....**(19)**.... my further admissions.

Thanking you

....**(20)**....

Muskan Gupta

Class X-C

18. (a) Permission to leave school
    (b) Application for School Leaving Certificate
    (c) Application for informing about leaving
    (d) Application to leave school

19. (a) Initiate
    (b) Astound
    (c) Conclude
    (d) Found

20. (a) Your lovingly
    (b) Your obediently
    (c) Your sincerely
    (d) Your faithfully

Communication Skills

1 Mark Questions

Directions (Q. Nos. 1-5) Select the correct word to fill the blanks.

1. A student to another student : Will our exams be conducted online .... offline?

    (a) and   (b) or   (c) either   (d) nor

2. Teacher to students : Please reach the venue 10 minutes .... the scheduled time.

    (a) after (b) between (c) early (d) before

3. Bus conductor to the passengers : Please wear your masks .... and take .... to purchase your tickets.

    (a) properly, turn   (b) loosely, turns
    (c) proper, turns   (d) properly, turns

4. Doctor : Please take .... safety precautions. Let's hope covid stops ....

    (a) some, spreading (b) all, spread
    (c) all, spreading   (d) any, spreading

5. Sohan to his father : Talking about the virus, what's the difference .... epidemic .... pandemic?

    (a) between, and   (b) in, and
    (c) between, or   (d) of, and

Directions (Q. Nos. 6-10) Complete the following conversations by choosing the correct word from the given options.

Sushil : Are you a new student here?

Kapil : Yes, I am. Are you a new student ...(6)...?

Sushil : No, ...(7)... been here for two months.

Kapil : Ok. What class ...(8)... in?

Sushil : Class III. I ...(9)... you are in class IV.

Kapil : You're right.

Sushil : ...(10)... is your class teacher?

Kapil : Mrs. Tandon, and your's?

6. (a) here   (b) two   (c) too   (d) now

7. (a) I had   (b) I have (c) I am   (d) I came

8. (a) you are   (b) you is
    (c) are your   (d) are you

9. (a) guess   (b) guessed
    (c) deny   (d) state

10. (a) What   (b) Who   (c) Where   (d) When

Directions (Q. Nos. 11-15) Complete the following conversations by choosing the correct word from the given options.

Pooja : Hello

Gargi : Hello. Is that Gunjan?

Pooja : Gunjan ? No. ...(11)... doesn't live here ...(12)... more.

Gargi : Oh! Do you know ...(13)... number?

Pooja : Yes. ...(14)... for a minute.

Gargi : Take your ...(15)...

11. (a) She   (b) She's
(c) He   (d) Her

12. (a) some   (b) any
(c) many   (d) not

13. (a) her's   (b) her know
(c) her new   (d) here new

14. (a) Please hold own
(b) Please hold down
(c) Please held on
(d) Please hold on

15. (a) times
(b) way
(c) time's
(d) time

Directions (Q.Nos. 16-18) Correct the underlined words in the following dialogues by replacing them with the correct one.

16. Prerna : Ma'am, <u>Can</u> I come in?

(a) Could   (b) May   (c) Would   (d) Shall

17. Rahul : Where are my car keys?
Pranjal : I gave it to you, <u>Had</u> I?
(a) Haven't I   (b) Did I
(c) Didn't I   (d) Do I

18. Rakul : Would you <u>minds share</u> your number with me?

Shobha : Not at all! Here it is.
(a) mind sharing   (b) better share
(c) minding share   (d) mind shares

2 Marks Questions

Directions (Q. Nos. 19-22) Choose the best answer to the following from the options given below.

19. Your friend tells you about a live show that she attended last night. Somehow, you were unable to attend and join her for the show. How will you respond to her?
(a) Was the show really interesting?
(b) I wish I'd gone with you.
(c) Who all performed at the show?
(d) All of the above

20. Aparajita : Is this Infosoft Technologies?

Receptionist : ....
(a) Don't you known it?
(b) Yes, I think so.
(c) Yes, What do you want?
(d) Yes, How may I help you?

21. Sonalika : Can you tell me when the online class will start?
Receptionist : ....
(a) Why don't you check on our website?
(b) It all depends on the chairman of this institute.
(c) Check the display board at our institute.
(d) The classes will start on 10th of this month.

22. You have to welcome the visitors for the annual function being held at your institute. You will say ....
(a) I'd like to welcome you all to our school function. It's a pleasure to have you here.
(b) Hmm...... It's good that you have come here to attend our annual function.
(c) It will be a great experience.
(d) You will soon be entertained by our participants.

PRACTICE SET 01

1 Mark Questions

Directions (Q. Nos. 1-5) Read the passage carefully and answer the questions that follow.

The most beautiful humming birds are found in the West Indies and South America. The crest of the tiny head of one of these shines like a sparkling crown of coloured light. The shades of colour that adorn its breast are equally brilliant. As the bird flits from one object to another, it looks more like a bright flash of sunlight than it does like a living being.

But, you ask, why are they called humming birds? It is because they make a soft, humming noise by the rapid motion of their wings — a motion so rapid, that as they fly, you can hardly see that they have wings.

One day when walking in the woods, I found the nest of one of the smallest humming birds. It was about half the size of a very small hen's egg and it was attached to a twig no thicker than a steel knitting needle. It seemed to have been made of cotton fibres and was covered with the softest bits of leaf and bark. It had two eggs in it and each was about as large as a small sugarplum.

When you <u>approach</u> the spot where one of these birds has built its nest, it is necessary to be careful. The mother bird will dart at you and try to peck your eyes. Its sharp beak may hurt your eyes most severely and even destroy your sight. The poor little thing knows no other way of defending its young and instinct teaches it that you might <u>carry off</u> its nest if you find it.

1. A humming bird's crest shines like a ....
   (a) diamond
   (b) gold
   (c) sparkling crown of coloured light
   (d) silver

2. Choose the correct statement.
   (a) The humming bird looks like a black cloud.
   (b) The humming bird looks like a bright flash of sunlight.
   (c) The humming bird looks as colourful as a dancing peacock.
   (d) The humming bird looks very clumsy while flying.

3. This bird is called 'humming bird' because ....
   (a) it is always singing
   (b) it makes a humming sound while feeding its children
   (c) it makes a humming noise by the rapid motion of its wings
   (d) it creates humming sound while hatching its eggs

4. The idiom 'carry off' used in the last paragraph means.
   (a) make the planned event successful
   (b) steal
   (c) borrow
   (d) take away

5. The antonym of the word 'approach' used in the last paragraph will be.
   - (a) access
   - (b) avenue
   - (c) leave
   - (d) advance

Directions (Q. Nos. 6 and 7) Fill in the blanks with suitable nouns from the options.

6. I don't have much ...., just two small bags.
   - (a) furniture
   - (b) trolley
   - (c) luggage
   - (d) room

7. The use of .... should be strictly prohibited in schools.
   - (a) books
   - (b) computers
   - (c) mobiles
   - (d) music

Directions (Q. Nos. 8 and 9) Fill in the blank with the correct tense of the verb from the given options.

8. The beautiful bungalow .... to a wealthy but eccentric man.
   - (a) is belonged
   - (b) been belonged
   - (c) has belonging
   - (d) belongs

9. My mother............ Dad's dinner in the microwave when he came back from office.
   - (a) has heating
   - (b) heated
   - (c) is heats
   - (d) did heating

Directions (Q. Nos. 10 and 11) Fill in the blanks by choosing suitable adjectives from the given options.

10. The weather forecast said there would be .... rain today.
   - (a) heavy
   - (b) more heavier
   - (c) heaviest
   - (d) None of these

11. Take plenty of exercise to keep your body ....
   - (a) healthful
   - (b) healthy
   - (c) active
   - (d) strong

Directions (Q. Nos. 12 and 13) Fill in the blanks by choosing appropriate prepositions from the options.

12. Helen is swimming .... the pool.
   - (a) over
   - (b) in
   - (c) below
   - (d) above

13. There are special containers for transporting goods .... rail.
   - (a) in
   - (b) from
   - (c) by
   - (d) with

Directions (Q. Nos. 14 and 15) Use a suitable conjunction to fill in the blank.

14. Send us the information on a postcard .... by courier.
   - (a) and
   - (b) or
   - (c) but
   - (d) so

15. I had planned to fly to Mauritius .... in the end I could not make it.
   - (a) so
   - (b) and
   - (c) or
   - (d) but

Directions (Q. Nos. 16 and 17) Change the following sentences into passive voice and choose the correct option.

16. Who taught you such things?
   - (a) Who was you taught such things by?
   - (b) She was taught such things by who?
   - (c) By whom you were taught such things?
   - (d) By whom were you taught such things?

17. A stone struck me on the head.
   - (a) I was struck on a stone by the head.
   - (b) My head was struck by a stone.
   - (c) I had been struck by a stone on the head.
   - (d) I was struck on the head by a stone.

Directions (Q. Nos. 18 and 19) Change the following sentences as directed. Choose from the options.

18. The noisy family shouted, "We have won a lottery!" (Change into indirect speech)
    (a) The noisy family said that they have won a lottery.
    (b) The noisy family exclaimed that they had won a lottery.
    (c) The noisy family told that they are winning a lottery.
    (d) The noisy family told every one that they would win a lottery.

19. The teacher ordered the boys to be quiet and do their class-work. (Change into Direct Speech)
    (a) The teacher requested, "Boys, be quiet and do your class-work."
    (b) The teacher said, "Be quiet, boys and do your class-work."
    (c) The teacher said, "Can you please be quiet boys and do your class-work?"
    (d) The teacher said, "Boys do your class work and be quiet."

Directions (Q. Nos. 20 and 21) Choose the correct synonym of the word underlined in the given sentences.

20. The mother <u>overruled</u> her son's demand for a motorbike.
    (a) neglected   (b) disallowed
    (c) ignored   (d) fulfilled

21. The story is too fantastic to be <u>credible</u>.
    (a) praiseworthy   (b) readable
    (c) false   (d) believable

Directions (Q. Nos. 22 and 23) Choose the correct antonym of the word underlined in the given sentences.

22. The flight was <u>delayed</u> because of bad weather.
    (a) hindered   (b) released
    (c) expedited   (d) triggered

23. The thief <u>confessed</u> at the police station that he had stolen my bag.
    (a) consented   (b) concealed
    (c) disapproved   (d) denied

Directions (Q. Nos. 24 and 25) Given below are four words. Three are similar in nature but one is different. Choose the odd one out.

24. (a) Gloves   (b) Socks
    (c) Stocking   (d) Raincoat

25. (a) Harmonium   (b) Guitar
    (c) Flute   (d) Piano

Directions (Q. Nos. 26 and 27) Choose the correctly punctuated sentence from the options.

26. (a) Mary shouted did you plan a tour to Mumbai last year
    (b) Mary asked, "Did you plan a tour to Mumbai last year"
    (c) Mary asked, "Did you plan a tour to Mumbai last year?"
    (d) Mary asked, "Did you plan a tour to Mumbai last year."

27. (a) Our Prime Minister Mr Narendra Modi is visiting many foreign countries these days.
    (b) Our Prime Minister, Mr. Narendra Modi, is visiting many foreign countries these days.
    (c) Our Prime Minister Mr Narendra Modi is visiting many foreign countries these day!
    (d) Our Prime Minister Mr Narendra Modi, is visiting many foreign countries these days?

Directions (Q. Nos. 28 and 29) Given below are words in a jumbled manner. Rearrange them to form a meaningful sentence. Choose from the options.

28. introduce / I'd / our / to / like / you / to / Meena / cook / new
    (a) I'd introduce you to like our new cook Meena.
    (b) I'd like you to introduce our new cook Meena.
    (c) I'd like to introduce you to our new cook Meena.
    (d) I'd like to introduce our new cook Meena to you.

29. to/again/we / seeing / forward / you / look
    (a) We look again forward seeing you.
    (b) We look forward to seeing you again.
    (c) We seeing forward to look you again.
    (d) We look forward seeing to you again.

Directions (Q. Nos. 30 and 31) Fill in the blank by choosing the correct word from the options.

30. The Principal .... the students on their performance.
    (a) complemented   (b) compleemented
    (c) complimented   (d) complimanted

31. Snoopy, our dog, is very naughty and often .... the furniture.
    (a) choose   (b) chose
    (c) chews   (d) choice

Directions (Q. Nos. 32-35) Given below is a telephonic conversation between Venkat and his sister. Based on this is given a message with some blanks. Fill in the blanks from the options given.

Venkat : Can I speak to mom?

Veena : She has gone out.

Venkat : I have to leave for Durgapur tomorrow at 4 a.m. for an Inter-School Football Match. Please ask, her to get my bag packed, as I will be back home late in the evening after practice.

Veena: I will.

Veena is going out for tuition so she writes a message.

6th July, 2015

2:30 p.m.

........(32)........,

Venkat called up to inform that he has to leave for ....(33)....... tomorrow at 4 a.m. for an ....(34)....... . You are requested to ......(35)...... . as he will return home late in the evening after practice.

Veena

32. (a) Dad   (b) Mom
    (c) Nani   (d) Sister

33. (a) Mumbai   (b) Patna
    (c) Bhagalpur   (d) Durgapur

34. (a) Inter-College Match
    (b) Inter-School Hockey Match
    (c) Inter-School Football Match
    (d) Inter-College Debate

35. (a) pack his lunch   (b) pack his clothes
    (c) pack his bag   (d) pack his suitcase

Directions (Q. Nos. 36-40) A letter is given below with some parts missing but substituted by numbers 36 to 40. Identify the missing parts. Choose the correct options to complete the letter.

132, Sahib Building,

Ajmer,

Rajasthan

6th July, 2015

Dear Mihir,

Your class teacher called me yesterday. She told me that you ....**(36)**....... . I was very glad to hear it. But she told me that you have become a computer addict and do not ....**(37)**....... in the evening. It is not good. It will ....**(38)**....... your health adversely.

I suggest you to ....**(39)**....... games. To be glued to the computer all the time is not ....**(40)**....... . It will affect your health as well as energy. Play any game for at least one hour. It will refresh your mind and keep you physically fit. This will also help you in your studies. Always remember the saying "work while you work and play while you play, that is the way to be happy."

With Love
Jackie

36. (a) were doing well in studies
    (b) are doing well in studies
    (c) are good in studies
    (d) are not doing well in your studies

37. (a) go out   (b) have any hobby
    (c) play any games   (d) do any thing else

38. (a) effect   (b) affect
    (c) harm   (d) damage

39. (a) take part in evening
    (b) participate in school
    (c) go out and play
    (d) pay attention of playing

40. (a) healthy   (b) good
    (c) constructive   (d) energisting

2 Marks Questions

41. Fill in the blanks with suitable option.
I saw many .... on the underside of a ....

    (a) lavva, leaf   (b) lavvae, leaves
    (c) larvae, leafs   (d) larvae, leaf

42. Consider the following statements.
1. She is talking to you and you are not listening to her.
2. He has been read a newspaper for two hours.
3. Did her daughter eat anything at all yesterday?

Which of these statements correctly uses verbs?

Codes
(a) 1 and 2
(b) 2 and 3
(c) 1 and 3
(d) Only 1

43. Match the following.

List I (Nouns)	List II (Adjectives)
A. Danger	1. Creative
B. Action	2. Dangerous
C. Creation	3. Active
D. Strength	4. Strong

Codes

	A	B	C	D			A	B	C	D
(a)	4	2	3	1		(b)	3	1	4	2
(c)	2	3	1	4		(d)	1	4	2	3

44. Which of these sentences have the correct usage of conjunction?
A. I tried to hit the nail but hit my thumb instead.
B. I would like a bike and commuting to work.
C. He not only but also studies hard works well.
D. She is very funny whereas he is boring.

Codes

(a) A and C   (b) B and C
(c) B and D   (d) A and D

45. Match the following.

List I (Word)		List II (Antonyms)
A.	Humiliate	1. Minimum
B.	Maximum	2. Dignify
C.	Ordinary	3. Unusual

Codes

	A	B	C			A	B	C
(a)	1	3	2		(b)	2	1	3
(c)	3	2	1		(d)	2	3	1

46. Match the following.

List I (Idiom/Phrases)		List II (Meaning)
A.	In the same boat	1. To succeed at something easily
B.	Pass with flying colours	2. Can't remember
C.	Draw a blank	3. In the same situation

Codes

	A	B	C			A	B	C
(a)	1	2	3		(b)	2	3	1
(c)	3	1	2		(d)	1	3	2

47. Fill in the blank of List I with a suitable preposition from List II to complete the sentences correctly.

List I		List II
A.	Pay attention .... what the teacher says.	1. on
B.	He is the man I was looking	2. upon
C.	The cat jumped .... the chair.	3. to
D.	The workers went .... strike to protest against the manager.	4. for

Codes

	A	B	C	D			A	B	C	D
(a)	2	4	3	1		(b)	4	2	1	3
(c)	3	4	2	1		(d)	2	3	4	1

48. Which of the following sentences have adverbs in them?

A. She suddenly started to lose control of her bodily functions.

B. Priya drew some squiggly lines on her draming sheet.

C. He usually goes for a walk after returning from office.

D. It's a rather cold day, isn't it?

Codes

(a) A and B   (b) B and C
(c) A and C   (d) B, C and D

49. Which of the following sentences have pronouns used incorrectly in them?

A. The group of students often stayed in one another's houses.

B. Amit and Drishti talk to one another regularly.

C. They stood up and clapped when it was over.

D. These are my friends Ruchi and Himanshu.

Codes

(a) Only D   (b) A and D
(c) Only C   (d) Only B

50. Read the given sentences and identify which of them are in active voice.

(i) The shopkeeper sells milk and butter.

(ii) The spider was killed by a lizard.

(iii) He was not invited in the party.

(iv) A letter was written to municipal commissioner.

Codes

(a) Only (iv)   (b) (ii) and (iii)
(c) Only (i)   (d) None of these

PRACTICE SET 02

1 Mark Questions

Directions (Q. Nos. 1-5) Read the passage carefully and answer the questions that follow.

Gold is the world's greatest treasure. People use it as money and wear it as jewellery. People and countries with lots of gold are considered rich and powerful. That is why monarchs wear golden crowns and important buildings have golden domes. Being a rare commodity, gold is valuable these days. Gold is a soft yellow metal. It is found throughout Earth in tiny amounts mixed with other rocks and minerals.

Gold is one of the least reactive metals. This means that compared to copper, silver and iron, it is less likely to react with the oxygen in the air. Copper turns green over time, silver turns black and iron rusts. Gold maintains its shine even after years of use. Even gold buried underground or underwater does not lose its value or <u>lustre</u>.

Gold is measured in units called carats. Pure gold is 24 carat gold. Each country sets its own standard for gold jewellery.

For thousands of years, gold has been used for money. Gold coins were common throughout the world at one time. Gold coins were used in Britain as far back as early AD 800. In the past, Asian rulers used gold more as jewellery and a form of decoration rather than currency.

They traded spices, silk and tea for Europe's gold. Today, much of the world's gold is stored as gold bars. Most countries keep a supply of gold bars that they can use to trade with other nations. This gold proves their wealth.

Today, it is a common practice in countries like India for personal wealth to be displayed by the gold they <u>adorn</u>. Indian women are known to take great pride in their collection.

1. Gold is considered to be valuable as it is
   ....
   (a) is uncommon
   (b) a rare commodity
   (c) can be used as jewellery
   (d) very expensive

2. The most special fact about gold is that
   ....
   (a) it may lose its shine after a period
   (b) it turns black after a few day's use
   (c) it can remain in its original state for a very long period of time
   (d) it can be measured in carats

3. The unit of measurement for gold is called
   ....
   (a) mole   (b) grain   (c) gram   (d) carat

4. The synonym of the word 'lustre' used in second paragraph of the passage will be
   ....
   (a) dullness   (b) polish
   (c) brightness   (d) darkness

5. The antonym of the word 'adorn' used in the last paragraph will be ....
   (a) furnish   (b) beautify
   (c) deform   (d) enhance

Directions (Q. Nos. 6 and 7) Fill in the blanks with suitable nouns.

6. Nivedita reads news on television. She is a ....
   - (a) proof reader
   - (b) publisher
   - (c) news reader
   - (d) editor

7. John draws the designs of buildings. He is a/an ....
   - (a) jeweller
   - (b) librarian
   - (c) astronaut
   - (d) architect

Directions (Q. Nos. 8 and 9) Find the odd one out.

8. (a) hut
   - (b) cottage
   - (c) hutch
   - (d) house

9. (a) cobbler
   - (b) sailor
   - (c) traitor
   - (d) watchman

Directions (Q. Nos. 10 and 11) Choose the correct verb to fill in the blanks.

10. The white shirt and the black trousers .... dirty.
    - (a) was
    - (b) were
    - (c) has
    - (d) is

11. The children .... trees in the school.
    - (a) has planting
    - (b) is planting
    - (c) are planting
    - (d) have planting

Directions (Q. Nos. 12 and 13) Fill in the blank by choosing the appropriate article from the options.

12. He knows what honour is but that does not make him .... honourable man.
    - (a) an
    - (b) the
    - (c) a
    - (d) this

13. As, I was walking back from school, I saw .... most unusual thing.
    - (a) a
    - (b) that
    - (c) an
    - (d) the

Directions (Q. Nos. 14 and 15) Choose suitable conjunction to fill the blanks.

14. .... I have had my lunch, I can still eat a pizza.
    - (a) However
    - (b) Moreover
    - (c) Although
    - (d) Already

15. I am not feeling well, ... I will come to the party.
    - (a) because (b) since (c) unless (d) but

Directions (Q. Nos. 16 and 17) Choose suitable preposition to fill the blanks.

16. Because we have no cars, we go everywhere .... foot.
    - (a) with (b) for (c) by (d) on

17. The pied piper stepped .... the street.
    - (a) over (b) into (c) under (d) upto

Directions (Q. Nos. 18 and 19) Change the voice of following sentences as directed.

18. They are building a house next door to our school (change into passive voice).
    - (a) A house next door to our school is being built by them.
    - (b) Next door to our school is being built a house by them.
    - (c) A house next door to our school is being built by them.
    - (d) A house is being built next door by them to our school.

19. Independence day was celebrated by the residents. (Change into active voice)
    - (a) The residents are celebrating Independence day.
    - (b) The residents celebrate Independence day.
    - (c) The residents celebrated Indepen- dence day.
    - (d) The residents have been celebrating Independence day.

Directions (Q. Nos. 20 and 21) Choose the correct synonym of the underlined phrase from the options.

20. I am busy, <u>hold on</u> for a minute.
(a) stay   (b) wait
(c) remain   (d) linger

21. After a long journey of 23 hours, he was completely <u>worn out</u>.
(a) sickened   (b) exhausted
(c) frail   (d) sleepy

Directions (Q. Nos. 22 and 23) Choose the word that is most nearly opposite of the given word.

22. Solitary
(a) Friendly   (b) Isolated
(c) Together   (d) Lonely

23. Consent
(a) Discard   (b) Surrender
(c) Approve   (d) dissent

24. Fill in the blank to complete the sentence in simple future tense.
Tomorrow the sun .... at 6:00 a.m.
(a) will rose   (b) will raise
(c) will risen   (d) will rise

25. Fill in the blank by choosing the appropriate adverb from the options
I am .... sorry for the inconvenience you are facing.
(a) quietly   (b) cruelly
(c) extremely   (d) entirely

Directions (Q. Nos. 26 and 27) Select the option which is punctuated correctly.

26. (a) We'll need a board counters and a pair of dice.
(b) We'll need a board, counters and a pair of dice.
(c) We'll need a board, counters and, a pair of dice.
(d) We'll need, a board, counters and a pair of dice.

27. (a) Sam asked, "Have I time to get popcorn", after he had bought his ticket.
(b) Sam asked, "Have I time to get popcorns after he had bought his ticket"?
(c) Sam asked, "Have I time to get popcorns?" after he had bought his ticket.
(d) Sam asked "have I time to get popcorns"! after he had bought his ticket.

Directions (Q. Nos. 28 and 29) Each question consists of two words which have a certain relationship to each other followed by four pairs of words. Select the most appropriate pair having the same relationship as the given pair.

28. Sight : Blind
(a) Language : Deaf
(b) Voice : Vibration
(c) Speech : Dumb
(d) Tongue : Sound

29. Distance : Kilometre
(a) Weight : Scale
(b) Present : Past
(c) Liquid : Litre
(d) Fame : Television

Directions (Q. Nos. 30 and 31) Fill the blanks by choosing the most suitable option.

30. Arrival : Departure : : .... : Death
(a) Person (b) Birth (c) Life (d) Train

31. Car : Road : : Train ....
(a) Vehicle   (b) Airstrip
(c) Wheel   (d) Track

Directions (Q. Nos. 32-35) Given below is an application by Anil Mehta to the school Principal to issue him a school leaving certificate as his father has been posted out of Delhi. Complete it by filling the blanks with the most suitable option given below.

The Principal

Navodaya School,

Lodhi Road,

New Delhi

8th July, 2015

Subject: ....**(32)**.......

Respected Sir,

This is to ....**(33)**....... you that my father is in a government job and has been ....**(34)**....... to Arunachal Pradesh. Thus, I will not be able ....**(35)**....... my studies in this school. Kindly issue me a school leaving certificate.

Thanking you

Respectfully yours

Anil Mehta,

Class V-B

32. (a) Issue of certificate
    (b) Request for school leaving certificate
    (c) Permission to leave the school
    (d) Allow to leave

33. (a) inform   (b) tell
    (c) put before   (d) intimate

34. (a) sent away   (b) flown
    (c) transferred   (d) gone

35. (a) to study here
    (b) to continue
    (c) to pursue
    (d) to carry on

Directions (Q. Nos. 36-40) Given below is a telephonic conversation between Kanu and Charu. Based on this a message has been written by Kanu. Fill in the blanks from the given options to complete the message.

Kanu : This is Kanu. May I know who is calling?

Charu : Hello, Kanu. This is Charu here. Is Bhavna at home?

Kanu : No, Charu, Bhavna has gone to her friend's house. She will be back after an hour or so.

Charu : All right; when she comes back, please tell her that I am going to Rehana's birthday party this evening. If Bhavna wants to go there, please tell her to be ready by 5:30 pm. I will pick her up.

Kanu : Don't worry. I'll convey the message. Anything else?

Charu : No thanks, bye.

Kanu is going out, so she writes a message for Bhavna

.......**(36)**.......

14th July, 2015

3:30 p.m.

Bhavna,

Your friend Charu called up ....**(37)**....... you that she is going to ....**(38)**....... this evening. She asked you ....**(39)**....... by 5:30 pm if you want to go. She will ....**(40)**........

Kanu

36. (a) Appeal
    (b) Notice
    (c) Message
    (d) E-mail

37. (a) telling   (b) to inform
    (c) to enquire   (d) to request

38. (a) her friend's house
    (b) watch a movie
    (c) Rehana's birthday party
    (d) farewell party

39. (a) to get ready
    (b) to buy some gifts
    (c) to give her money
    (d) to be ready

40. (a) escort you   (b) take you
    (c) call you   (d) pick you up

2 Marks Questions

41. Fill in the blank with the correct option.
Ratnesh .... that you ....
(a) will think, mistake
(b) thought, mistook
(c) think, mistake
(d) thinks, are mistaken

42. Fill in the blanks with the correct pronoun to complete the sentence given.

.... decided to approach the Principal .... as our teacher did not do so.
(a) We, myself
(b) We, ourselves
(c) She, themselves
(d) He, ourself

43. Read the passage given below and fill in the blanks with suitable adjectives.
One .... day, my little puppy jumped onto our red couch and played with his .... toy. I liked to watch him play and it made me happy. Soon, my .... puppy yawned. I picked him up and laid him on his ...., round bed and he slept.
(a) Sun, old, play, hard
(b) Sunny, old, play, soft
(c) Sunny, new, playful, soft
(d) Sun, new, playful, hard

44. Choose the option with the correct meaning of the idiom underlined in the sentence given below.

He was always a <u>black sheep</u> in the community due to his intoxication with drugs.
(i) A person who causes shame or embarrassment
(ii) Owner of a black coloured sheep
(iii) Dark-skinned person
(iv) Most virtuous character
Codes
(a) Only (i)
(b) (i) and (iii)
(c) (ii) and (iv)
(d) None of these

Directions (Q. Nos. 45 and 46) Find the correct abstract noun in the given sentences.

45. Soldiers fight on the borders with full dedication for their country.
A. Fight   B. Country
C. Soldiers   D. Dedication
(a) A and B   (b) Only D
(c) Only B   (d) C and D

46. Both men and women are working hard to live a better life.
A. Both   B. Men and women
C. Better   D. Life
(a) A and C
(b) B and D
(c) Only A
(d) Only D

47. Which of the following statements use correct pronoun?

Statement (P) : These gifts are for you and me.

Statement (Q) : These gifts are for you and I.

Statement (R) : My brother and I are going to Delhi.

Statement (S) : My brother and myself are going to Delhi.

Codes

(a) (P) and (Q) are correct

(b) (Q) and (S) are correct

(c) (R) and (S) are correct

(d) (P) and (R) are correct

48. Which of the following sentences is/are in past perfect tense?

A. Had the water boiled when you went to kitchen?

B. Mark has studied two foreign languages.

C. I lived in London before moving to Paris.

D. The baby had cried before her father came.

Codes

(a) Only A   (b) A and C

(c) B and D   (d) A and D

49. Select the sentence in which adverb "usually" appears in an appropriate position.

(a) She usually shops for clothes at the local thrift store.

(b) Usually, she shops for clothes at the local thrift store.

(c) She shops for clothes at the local thrift store usually.

(d) Either A or B.

50. Choose the correctly punctuated sentences.

Statement A : Jack, Jill and Bob went up the hill; the last watched the other two fall down.

Statement B : The former half of the film is more interesting than the latter half said Rohit.

Statement C : "Clean your feet before you enter said claire."

Codes

(a) A and B

(b) A and C

(c) Only A

(d) B and C

ANSWERS

Chapter 1 Nouns

1. (c)	**2.** (d)	**3.** (d)	**4.** (b)	**5.** (d)	**6.** (b)	**7.** (b)	**8.** (c)	**9.** (b)	**10.** (b)
11. (c)	**12.** (c)	**13.** (c)	**14.** (b)	**15.** (a)	**16.** (a)	**17.** (b)	**18.** (b)	**19.** (a)	**20.** (c)
21. (a)	**22.** (b)	**23.** (b)	**24.** (c)	**25.** (d)					

Chapter 2 Pronouns

1. (d)	**2.** (d)	**3.** (a)	**4.** (d)	**5.** (c)	**6.** (b)	**7.** (c)	**8.** (d)	**9.** (b)	**10.** (c)
11. (b)	**12.** (d)	**13.** (b)	**14.** (b)	**15.** (d)	**16.** (a)	**17.** (c)	**18.** (a)	**19.** (c)	**20.** (b)
21. (b)	**22.** (a)	**23.** (b)	**24.** (a)	**25.** (b)	**26.** (a)	**27.** (b)	**28.** (a)	**29.** (c)	**30.** (d)

Chapter 3 Verb

1. (b)	**2.** (b)	**3.** (c)	**4.** (c)	**5.** (a)	**6.** (a)	**7.** (d)	**8.** (a)	**9.** (b)	**10.** (b)
11. (b)	**12.** (c)	**13.** (b)	**14.** (c)	**15.** (d)	**16.** (a)	**17.** (c)	**18.** (d)	**19.** (c)	**20.** (a)

Chapter 4 Adverbs

1. (d)	**2.** (b)	**3.** (a)	**4.** (b)	**5.** (b)	**6.** (d)	**7.** (c)	**8.** (d)	**9.** (c)	**10.** (c)
11. (c)	**12.** (d)	**13.** (d)	**14.** (b)	**15.** (a)	**16.** (a)	**17.** (d)	**18.** (d)	**19.** (d)	**20.** (c)

Chapter 5 Adjectives

1. (c)	**2.** (b)	**3.** (c)	**4.** (c)	**5.** (b)	**6.** (b)	**7.** (b)	**8.** (d)	**9.** (c)	**10.** (b)
11. (a)	**12.** (b)	**13.** (b)	**14.** (a)	**15.** (c)	**16.** (b)	**17.** (d)	**18.** (c)	**19.** (c)	**20.** (a)
21. (c)	**22.** (c)	**23.** (b)	**24.** (d)	**25.** (c)					

Chapter 6 Articles

1. (a)	**2.** (c)	**3.** (b)	**4.** (c)	**5.** (d)	**6.** (c)	**7.** (d)	**8.** (d)	**9.** (a)	**10.** (c)
11. (b)	**12.** (a)	**13.** (b)	**14.** (d)	**15.** (b)	**16.** (d)	**17.** (d)	**18.** (d)	**19.** (c)	**20.** (b)

21. (b) **22.** (c) **23.** (i) (c), (ii) (a), (iii) (b), (iv) (a), (v) (b) **24.** (b) **25.** (d)

26. (i) (b), (ii) (a), (iii) (d), (iv) (c), (v) (c), (vi) (a)

Chapter 7 Prepositions

1. (c)	**2.** (c)	**3.** (b)	**4.** (c)	**5.** (b)	**6.** (b)	**7.** (b)	**8.** (b)	**9.** (b)	**10.** (d)
11. (b)	**12.** (b)	**13.** (a)	**14.** (c)	**15.** (a)	**16.** (c)	**17.** (d)	**18.** (b)	**19.** (a)	**20.** (a)
21. (d)	**22.** (a)	**23.** (d)	**24.** (c)	**25.** (d)	**26.** (a)	**27.** (d)	**28.** (c)	**29.** (d)	

30. (i) (c) (ii) (d) (iii) (c) (iv) (b) (v) (a)

Chapter 8   Conjunctions

1. (d)	**2.** (b)	**3.** (d)	**4.** (c)	**5.** (d)	**6.** (c)	**7.** (d)	**8.** (c)	**9.** (c)	**10.** (d)
11. (d)	**12.** (d)	**13.** (b)	**14.** (c)	**15.** (d)	**16.** (a)	**17.** (d)	**18.** (b)	**19.** (c)	**20.** (a)
21. (b)	**22.** (c)	**23.** (d)	**24.** (c)	**25.** (i) (a), (ii) (b), (iii) (d), (iv) (b)					

Chapter 9   Sentences

1. (c)	**2.** (a)	**3.** (b)	**4.** (d)	**5.** (a)	**6.** (d)	**7.** (c)	**8.** (a)	**9.** (d)	**10.** (b)
11. (b)	**12.** (d)	**13.** (d)	**14.** (a)	**15.** (c)	**16.** (a)	**17.** (d)	**18.** (c)	**19.** (b)	**20.** (a)

Chapter 10   Tenses

1. (c)	**2.** (d)	**3.** (c)	**4.** (b)	**5.** (b)	**6.** (b)	**7.** (c)	**8.** (a)	**9.** (b)	**10.** (c)
11. (a)	**12.** (b)	**13.** (c)	**14.** (c)	**15.** (a)	**16.** (c)	**17.** (c)	**18.** (c)	**19.** (c)	**20.** (a)
21. (a)	**22.** (c)	**23.** (d)	**24.** (d)	**25.** (a)	**26.** (d)	**27.** (d)			

Chapter 11   Punctuations

1. (d)	**2.** (c)	**3.** (a)	**4.** (b)	**5.** (d)	**6.** (a)	**7.** (b)	**8.** (d)	**9.** (c)	**10.** (a)
11. (b)	**12.** (d)	**13.** (b)	**14.** (c)	**15.** (i) (a), (ii) (d)	**16.** (b)	**17.** (d)	**18.** (d)	**19.** (b)	**20.** (c)
21. (c)	**22.** (d)								

Chapter 12   Active and Passive Voice

1. (c)	**2.** (b)	**3.** (b)	**4.** (a)	**5.** (c)	**6.** (c)	**7.** (a)	**8.** (c)	**9.** (d)	**10.** (b)
11. (c)	**12.** (a)	**13.** (a)	**14.** (d)	**15.** (c)	**16.** (a)	**17.** (c)	**18.** (c)		

Chapter 13   Direct and Indirect Speech

1. (b)	**2.** (c)	**3.** (d)	**4.** (d)	**5.** (b)	**6.** (a)	**7.** (d)	**8.** (d)	**9.** (d)	**10.** (a)
11. (b)	**12.** (c)	**13.** (a)	**14.** (c)	**15.** (d)	**16.** (d)	**17.** (a)	**18.** (a)		
19. (i) (b), (ii) (b) (iii) (b)									

Chapter 14   Synonyms and Antonyms

1. (b)	**2.** (c)	**3.** (b)	**4.** (a)	**5.** (d)	**6.** (b)	**7.** (c)	**8.** (b)	**9.** (b)	**10.** (c)
11. (c)	**12.** (b)	**13.** (b)	**14.** (d)	**15.** (c)	**16.** (c)	**17.** (d)	**18.** (d)	**19.** (c)	**20.** (b)
21. (c)	**22.** (c)	**23.** (b)	**24.** (c)	**25.** (d)					

Chapter 15   Homophones and Homonyms

1. (b)	**2.** (a)	**3.** (a)	**4.** (c)	**5.** (c)	**6.** (c)	**7.** (b)	**8.** (d)	**9.** (b)	**10.** (c)
11. (b)	**12.** (a)	**13.** (b)	**14.** (c)	**15.** (a)	**16.** (d)	**17.** (d)	**18.** (b)	**19.** (c)	**20.** (d)
21. (c)	**22.** (d)								

Chapter 16   One Word Substitution

1. (b)	**2.** (b)	**3.** (a)	**4.** (d)	**5.** (c)	**6.** (d)	**7.** (d)	**8.** (d)	**9.** (b)	**10.** (c)
11. (b)	**12.** (a)	**13.** (c)	**14.** (c)	**15.** (d)	**16.** (d)				

Chapter 17　Idioms and Phrases

1. (c)	2. (c)	3. (a)	4. (d)	5. (d)	6. (c)	7. (b)	8. (a)	9. (d)	10. (b)
11. (d)	12. (c)	13. (c)	14. (b)	15. (b)	16. (b)	17. (a)	18. (c)	19. (b)	20. (b)
21. (c)	22. (a)								

Chapter 18　Jumbled Words and Sentences

1. (d)	2. (c)	3. (a)	4. (d)	5. (c)	6. (a)	7. (b)	8. (b)	9. (c)	10. (c)
11. (b)	12. (a)	13. (c)	14. (b)	15. (b)	16. (c)	17. (b)			

Chapter 19　Spelling Test

1. (b)	2. (d)	3. (d)	4. (a)	5. (c)	6. (a)	7. (d)	8. (d)	9. (b)	10. (b)
11. (a)	12. (c)	13. (a)	14. (d)	15. (d)	16. (b)	17. (d)	18. (c)	19. (c)	20. (b)
21. (d)	22. (a)	23. (d)	24. (d)	25. (c)	26. (c)	27. (d)	28. (c)	29. (d)	30. (a)
31. (b)	32. (c)								

Chapter 20　Reading Comprehension

1. (c)	2. (d)	3. (b)	4. (b)	5. (b)	6. (c)	7. (d)	8. (b)	9. (c)	10. (b)
11. (b)	12. (a)	13. (b)	14. (c)	15. (d)	16. (a)	17. (c)	18. (b)	19. (d)	

Chapter 21　Writing Skills

1. (c)	2. (d)	3. (c)	4. (b)	5. (b)	6. (b)	7. (d)	8. (c)	9. (c)	10. (d)
11. (b)	12. (c)	13. (b)	14. (d)	15. (d)	16. (a)	17. (b)	18. (b)	19. (a)	20. (b)

Chapter 22　Communication Skills

1. (b)	2. (d)	3. (d)	4. (c)	5. (a)	6. (c)	7. (b)	8. (d)	9. (a)	10. (b)
11. (a)	12. (b)	13. (c)	14. (d)	15. (d)	16. (b)	17. (c)	18. (a)	19. (d)	20. (d)
21. (d)	22. (a)								

Practice Set 1

1. (c)	2. (b)	3. (c)	4. (d)	5. (c)	6. (c)	7. (c)	8. (d)	9. (b)	10. (a)
11. (b)	12. (b)	13. (c)	14. (b)	15. (d)	16. (d)	17. (d)	18. (b)	19. (b)	20. (b)
21. (d)	22. (c)	23. (d)	24. (d)	25. (c)	26. (c)	27. (b)	28. (c)	29. (b)	30. (c)
31. (c)	32. (b)	33. (d)	34. (c)	35. (c)	36. (b)	37. (c)	38. (b)	39. (c)	40. (b)
41. (d)	42. (c)	43. (c)	44. (d)	45. (b)	46. (c)	47. (c)	48. (c)	49. (d)	50. (c)

Practice Set 2

1. (b)	2. (c)	3. (d)	4. (c)	5. (c)	6. (c)	7. (d)	8. (c)	9. (c)	10. (b)
11. (c)	12. (a)	13. (d)	14. (c)	15. (d)	16. (d)	17. (b)	18. (c)	19. (c)	20. (b)
21. (b)	22. (c)	23. (d)	24. (d)	25. (c)	26. (b)	27. (c)	28. (c)	29. (c)	30. (b)
31. (d)	32. (b)	33. (a)	34. (c)	35. (b)	36. (c)	37. (b)	38. (c)	39. (d)	40. (d)
41. (d)	42. (b)	43. (c)	44. (a)	45. (b)	46. (d)	47. (d)	48. (d)	49. (d)	50. (a)